Environmental Activism and the Maternal

Mothers and Mother Earth in Activism and Discourse

T0294110

Edited by Rebecca Jaremko Bromwich, Noemie Richard, Olivia Ungar, Melanie Younger and Maryellen Symons

DEMETER

Environmental Activism and the Maternal

Mothers and Mother Earth in Activism and Discourse

Edited by Rebecca Jaremko Bromwich, Noemie Richard, Olivia Ungar, Melanie Younger and Maryellen Symons

Demeter Press
2546 10th Line
Bradford, Ontario
Canada, L3Z 3L3
Tel: 289-383-0134
Email: info@demeterpress.org
Website: www.demeterpress.org

Demeter Press logo based on the sculpture "Demeter" by Maria-Luise Bodirsky www.keramik-atelier.bodirsky.de

Printed and Bound in Canada

Front cover artwork: *Baby New Year Plastic World* by Dara Herman Zierlein
Cover design and typesetting: Michelle Pirovich

Library and Archives Canada Cataloguing in Publication
Title: Environmental activism and the maternal : Mothers and Mother Earth in activism and discourse / edited by Rebecca Jaremko Bromwich, Noemie Richard, Maryellen Symons, Olivia Ungar, and Melanie Younger.
Names: Bromwich, Rebecca, editor. | Richard, Noemie, 1999- editor. | Symons, Maryellen, 1939- editor. | Ungar, Olivia, 1997- editor. | Younger, Melanie, 1982- editor.
Description: Includes bibliographical references.
Identifiers: Canadiana 20200257390 | ISBN 9781772582321 (softcover)
Subjects: LCSH: Ecofeminism. | LCSH: Women and the environment. | LCSH: Women environmentalists. | LCSH: Mothers. | LCSH: Motherhood.
Classification: LCC HQ1194.E58 2020 | DDC 304.2082—dc23

Acknowledgments

The contributors to this volume owe a debt of gratitude to Demeter Press and Andrea O'Reilly for providing a space for this work by publishing it. Nothing grows but in good soil; no work comes to fruition without support. We all wish also to acknowledge our own mothers as well as our families, colleagues, and friends for supporting us in this work.

Contents

CONTENTS

Environmental Activism and the Maternal: Mothers and Mother Earth in Activism and Discourse

Rebecca Jaremko Bromwich, Ozkan Ozcevik,
Maryellen Symons, Melanie Younger, and Olivia Ungar

"This is really why I made my daughters learn to garden—so they would always have a mother to love them, long after I am gone."

—Robin Wall Kimmerer

In environmental activism, and climate activism in particular, maternal thinking about the wellbeing of future children, as well as the personification of Mother Earth, is frequently invoked. Activists involved in environmental advocacy are often mothers, and, moreover, many women within environmental justice serve as mothers to movements. These women may or may not have birthed children, but they play foundational roles in giving birth to ideas and in nurturing revolution through their thoughts, actions, creations, and community tending. These women embody motherhood through their roles as community leaders and through the emotional, domestic, and political labour they share with those they work alongside. Connections between representations of the maternal, mothering, and environmental activism are understudied in academic work. This anthology has been curated to fill this gap and bring together a diverse range of scholarly and creative contributions themed around mothers, mothering, and environmental activism.

This anthology seeks to explore the complex, varied, and sometimes contradictory intersections between mothers, mothering, and environmental activism in discourse and in lived experiences. It looks critically, yet hopefully, at the ways in which feminist, Indigenous, and environmentalist challenges to the Western, capitalist moral imagination are linked. The collection explores the impact of rape culture and the ways in which a capitalist, patriarchal society interacts with the earth as a feminine-personified identity. It also shares the hope of raising the consciousness of the next generation of women and their ability to effect change. This work endeavours to share lessons from the earth in resistance to the continued assaults of anthropogenic capitalist industry and to inspire new ways to resist, rise up, and revolt as mothers and as women.

This volume is a space for critical discussion about representations linking environmental activism, maternality, and Mother Earth as well as a venue for creative expression and art. In keeping with its intention to provide a space for discussing a complex and varied array of perspectives on mothers, mothering, and Mother Earth, this is an interdisciplinary anthology. The contributors come from a wide range of disciplines and fields, including psychology, sociology, anthropology, women's and gender studies, cultural studies, literary studies, as well as law and legal studies. The contributions from scholars working in the social sciences are interwoven with creative contributions from academics, writers, and artists working in the humanities. Although the contributions contained within this book have a shared interest in environmental sustainability, this anthology offers no single, unified, or monolithic position on activism in relation to Mother Earth; rather, it provides a space for exploring the complex relationship between environmental activism and representations of the maternal in a transnational, intersectional context.

This anthology contributes to the fields of environmental activism, the feminist study of environmentalist thought, as well as feminist ethics relating to environmental sustainability, which are well-developed areas of literature (Zimmerman). Problems relating to environmental justice have been critically understood for many years as problems of inequality and oppression (Adamson et al.). Since the second-wave beginnings of ecofeminism (Gaard), feminist writers have connected constructs of femininity to the natural environment, whether critically or essentially

(Caldecott). This text also draws on prior writing about Indigenous constructions of Mother Earth in grassroots environmental activism (Clarke).

Literature Review

A rich and varied literature has developed that engages with issues of gender, equality, maternality, and environmental conservation in a wide variety of ways. Noted below are some important works in this regard.

Naomi Klein's *This Changes Everything: Capitalism vs. the Climate* (2015) is an important contribution to the discussion of strategy and tactics for climate action. This book covers a lot of bases concerning the importance of climate change as an issue demanding concerted action. It also looks at the contributing social forces, the mythology behind frequently touted remedies, the state of the environmental and climate action movements, and possibilities for organizing an effective mass movement.

In *Braiding Sweetgrass: Indigenous Wisdom, Scientific Knowledge and the Teachings of Plants* (2013), Robin Wall Kimmerer weaves together Indigenous knowledge, plant science, and personal narrative. Kimmerer is a mother, a scientist, a decorated professor, and a member of the Citizen Potawatomi Nation. As a botanist, Kimmerer has been trained to ask questions of nature through a lens of scientific inquiry. She also embraces the Indigenous worldview that plants and animals are our oldest teachers. In Kimmerer's book, these two lenses of knowledge come together.

In *Earth Democracy: Justice, Sustainability and Peace* (2006), environmental activist and physicist Vandana Shiva calls for a radical shift in the values that govern democracies, as she condemns the role that unrestricted capitalism has played in the destruction of environments and livelihoods. She explores issues including genetic food engineering, culture theft, and natural resource privatization while uncovering their links to violence against women and climate change.

Joanna Macy's *Greening of the Self* (2013) explores the premise that individuals are not separated from the world. Instead, they are always what Macy calls "co-arising" or cocreating the world, and, as such, they cannot escape the consequences resulting from environment degradation. Macy argues that by broadening our view of what constitutes the "self" to include an environmental relationship, a new "ecological self" may emerge.

Living on the Land: Indigenous Women's Understanding of Place (2016) examines how patriarchy, gender, and colonialism have shaped the experiences of Indigenous women as both knowers and producers of knowledge. From a variety of methodological perspectives, contributors to the volume explore the nature and scope of Indigenous women's knowledge, its rootedness in relationships, both human and spiritual, and its inseparability from the land.

Spiritual Ecology: The Cry of the Earth (2013), edited by Llewellyn Vaughan-Lee, highlights the deep connection between the present ecological crisis and the lack of awareness concerning the sacred nature of creation. This series of essays from spiritual and environmental leaders around the world shows how humanity can transform its relationship with the earth.

In *Field Notes from a Catastrophe: Man, Nature, and Climate Change* (2015), Elizabeth Kolbert methodically explains the science of climate change while highlighting the earth's rising temperature. She takes the reader on a journey beginning in the interior of Alaska to discuss the thawing of the permafrost and how this indicates a rise in global temperatures. She then travels to the ice sheets of Greenland and to the jungles of Costa Rica speaking with scientists, and she paints a shocking picture of how quickly the earth is warming and what the consequences will be for the many species who are on the brink of extinction and, of course, for humans and the world as well

The End of Nature (2006) by Bill McKibben is an impassioned plea for radical and life-renewing change and is considered a groundbreaking work in environmental studies. McKibben argues that the survival of the Earth is dependent on a fundamental, philosophical shift in the way humans relate to nature.

Susan Griffin's *Woman and Nature: The Roaring Inside Her* (2016) explores the identification of women with the earth both as sustenance for humanity and as victim of male rage. To show how patriarchal Western philosophy and religion have used language and science to bolster their power over both women and nature, she draws on a diverse range of sources from timbering manuals to medical texts to scripture and classical literature.

Sister Species: Women, Animals and Social Justice (2011), edited by Lisa A. Kemmerer, addresses the interconnections between speciesism, sexism, racism, and homophobia, and clarifies why social justice activists

in the twenty-first century must challenge intersecting forms of oppression. These essays highlight how women have always been important
to social justice and animal advocacy, and they urge the reader to
recognize the links that continue to bind all oppressed individuals.

Ecofeminism (2014) by Maria Mies and Vandana Shiva presents a feminist epistemology as well as builds a theoretical framework that sheds
light on the connection between the subjugation of women and the
exploitation of nature by capitalist and patriarchal hegemonies.

Val Plumwood's *Feminism and the Mastery of Nature* (1993) is often
regarded as a foundational ecofeminist work. In her feminist critique of
reason, Plumwood singles out the dualistic mode of thinking that per-
meates the history of Western thought. She further argues that this
patriarchal and dualistic form of rationality has served to sustain the
exploitation of various social groups and nature at the hands of what
Plumwood calls the "master" identities that have been dominant
throughout history. Plumwood updates her critique in *Environmental
Culture: The Ecological Crisis of Reason* (2002), in which she investigates
in detail the connections between contemporary society and today's ecological crisis.

In her book *The Death of Nature: Women, Ecology, and the Scientific
Revolution* (1980), Carolyn Merchant challenges the normative hegemony
of mechanistic science. She argues that what is integral to the scientific
method of the seventeenth century is the androcentric ideal of subjugation
of nature as female. The prevailing depiction of nature as feminine,
Merchant maintains, is doubly problematic because it has contributed
to the historical subjugation of women as well as to today's environmental
crisis.

In *Ecofeminist Philosophy,* (2002) Karen J. Warren puts forward some
of the most compelling arguments for ecofeminism. Unlike early ecofeminists, Warren takes care to avoid essentialist arguments and instead
identifies "nature" and "woman" as social constructs of a patriarchal
society. This book offers an expansive critique of various types of oppression and exploitation prevalent today. According to Warren, these
multifarious forms must all be seen as feminist issues because understanding any one of them will invariably help us to understand the per-
sisting subjugation of women.

While it connects with well-developed fields of study and creative
endeavour, what makes this anthology unique, in addition to the fact

that it presents contributions from a diverse range of disciplines and creative fields brought together in an unusual way, is its specific consideration of the intersection of maternal feminist thought and environmental activism. It is in its particular attention to mothering, motherhood, and theories and discourses of maternality that this book fills a unique gap in existing literature.

Maternal Feminist Scholarship

This book is situated within the field of maternal feminist scholarship and specifically what Andrea O'Reilly has termed "matricentric feminism," which encompasses feminist scholarship about motherhood as well as activism that seeks the equality of mothers as a category of persons with other human beings. Matricentric feminism has dimensions rooted in theory, activism and practice, and it is grounded in the theoretical work of Sara Ruddick, and her theory of maternal thinking, as well as Adrienne Rich. It is politically engaged scholarship, which is committed to the attainment of equality and the ending of oppression for mothers, and it also involves practices of feminist parenting that support the humanity of parents and children alike.

This book is unique also in that although it contains contributions from a wide range of geographical contexts, it particularly focuses on Canadian environmental activism and on that country's laws, institutions, circumstances, and mothers. This book seeks to contextualize the experiences of mothers with environmental activism and to critically unpack representations of the maternal in dialogues and debates about environmental conservation. It situates those in political and social systems where the oppression of women, and in particular of mothers, remains a significant influence on their lives.

The Contributions

Chapter 1, by Anishinaabe academic and writer Renée E. Mazinegiizhigookwe Bédard, explores Anishinaabe-kwewag maternal environmental activism as well as the connection between her Nation's culture and environmental advocacy and activism. The chapter mainly focuses on Anishinaabe women's traditional responsibilities in regard to the earth and water (Aki and Nibi, respectively). The cultural relationship between women and the water is described as an integral part of life, reproduction, and birth, which is also deserving of nourishment. The chapter provides rich feminist and Indigenous narratives about the relationships between mothers, women, and the environment.

In Chapter 2, Rebecca Bromwich critically discusses how the personification of earth and nature as maternal has been deployed in the Keystone XL pipeline debate. Her chapter considers how maternal understandings of the earth have potential to be problematic in the fight towards a healthier environment. She uses critical discourse analysis to explore the implications of the gendering and maternalizing imaginings of the earth. Through feminist, Indigenous, and legal lenses, the chapter explores how the phrase "Mother Earth" is used in relation to the exploitative practices associated with the construction of the Keystone XL pipeline.

In Chapter 3, Karen I. Case narrates and analyzes the works of Almira Hart Lincoln Phelps, a nineteenth-century botanist. Her paper describes the life of Almira and her struggles as a woman in her time as well as the path she carved for women today, being an incredibly successful author and botanist.

In Chapter 4, Nurcan Atalan-Helicke explores food security in Turkey, specifically the role of mothers in providing food for their children, unpacking the emotions and experiences surrounding that traditionally maternal job. The author also discusses GMOs (genetically modified organisms) in relation to the consumer habits of mothers in Turkey and the attitudes that surround GMO versus more natural foods. The chapter also addresses such issues as food scarcity and food movements in Turkey and how mothers react to them.

In Chapter 5, Dwayne Avery discusses postapocalyptic cinema and how environmental disaster is portrayed. Avery analyzes the maternal personification of nature in these films and critiques the problematic message such a depiction entails. The chapter seeks to address the complicated role gender plays in the environmental advocacy presented in these films.

Chapter 6 features environmentally themed creative writing by criminologist Josephine Savarese, and Chapter 7 is author Laura Wythe's contribution, a fictional narrative excerpted from her book, *The Bones*, that follows the flashbacks of a girl who is seeing her life in a series of mundane, yet typically female, tasks on a farm and memories of her life as a young girl, which turns unfortunately tragic.

Finally, Chapter 8 contains two companion contributions: a painting by Alberta artist Janet Fraser of a tree is presented together with a poem written one hundred years ago by her grandmother, Northern Alberta school teacher Blanche MacDonald Markstad, who was one of the area's first European settler pioneers. This volume, which begins with writing by an Indigenous scholar, concludes with historical writing and art of European settlers, intending to trouble, through this contrast, contemporary western worldviews of nature, the environment, and the maternal. Interwoven throughout this collection is artwork by Dara Herman Zierlein—a political artist whose work focuses on social justice, human and animal rights, women and equal rights, and plastic pollution—as well as an illustration by Andromeda Bromwich.

Works Cited

Adamson, Joni, Mei Mei Evans, and Rachel Stein, editors. *The Environmental Justice Reader: Politics, Poetics, and Pedagogy.* The University of Arizona Press, 2002.

Caldecott, Leonie and Stephanie Leland, editors. *Reclaim the Earth: Women Speak Out for Life on Earth.* Women's Press, 1983.

Clarke, Chris. "Defending Mother Earth: Native American Perspectives on Environmental Justice" *Ecotheology.* Vol. 7, July 1999, pp. 118-120.

Gaard, Greta, editor. *Ecofeminism: Women, Animals, Nature.* Temple University Press, 1993.

Griffin, Susan. *Woman and Nature: The Roaring Inside Her.* Counterpoint, 2016.

Kemmerer, Lisa A., editor. *Sister Species: Women, Animals, and Social Justice.* University of Illinois Press, 2011.

Kimmerer, Robin Wall. *Braiding Sweetgrass: Indigenous Wisdom, Scientific Knowledge and the Teachings of Plants.* Milkweed Editions, 2013.

Klein, Naomi. *This Changes Everything: Capitalism vs. the Climate.* Simon and Schuster, 2015.

Kolbert, Elizabeth. *Field Notes from a Catastrophe: Man, Nature, and Climate Change.* Bloomsbury Publishing USA, 2015.

Macy, Joanna. *Greening of the Self.* Parallax Press, 2013.

McKibben, Bill. *The End of Nature.* Random House Incorporated, 2006.

Merchant, Carolyn. *The Death of Nature: Women, Ecology, and Scientific Revolution.* 1980. HarperCollins, 1990.

Mies, Maria, and Vandana Shiva. *Ecofeminism,* 2nd ed. Zed Books Ltd., 2014.

O'Reilly, Andrea. *Matricentric Feminism: Theory, Activism, Practice.* Demeter Press, 2016.

Plumwood, Val. *Feminism and the Mastery of Nature.* Routledge, 1993.

Plumwood, Val. *Environmental Culture: The Ecological Crisis of Reason.* Routledge, 2002.

Rich, Adrienne. *Of Woman Born: Motherhood as Experience and Institution.* Norton, 1995.

Ruddick, Sara. *Maternal Thinking: Towards a Politics of Peace.* Beacon Press, 1995.

Shiva, Vandana. *Earth Democracy: Justice, Sustainability, and Peace.* Zed Books, 2006.

Vaughan-Lee, Llewellyn, editor. *Spiritual Ecology: The Cry of the Earth.* The Golden Sufi Center, 2013.

Warren, Karen. *Ecofeminist Philosophy: A Western Perspective on What It Is and Why It Matters.* Rowman & Littlefield, 2000.

Zimmerman, Michael. "Feminism, Deep Ecology, and Environmental Ethics." *Environmental Ethics* vol. 9, no.1, 1987, pp. 21-44.

Part I

Mother Earth in Indigenous Frameworks

Chapter One

Anishinaabe-Kwewag Mothers, the Environment, and Maternal Discourse on Responsibilities to Aki (Earth) and Nibi (Water): Anishinaabe-Kwewag Maternal Environmental Activism

Renée E. Mazinegiizhigoo-kwe Bédard

Niibiwa Mino Gikinoo'amaage Akiing (The Many Good Teachings of the Land)

Boozhoo indinawemaaganag! Greetings my all relatives!
Mzinegiizhigo-kwe indanishinaabewinikaazowin. Ozhibii'iweg
and Nibiising Anishinaabe-kwe ndaaw. Waabizheshii niin
ndoondem. I'iwidi ayi'iing, agaami-zaaga'igan Waabnoong
Bemjwang imaa Okikendawdt miinawaa Nibiinsing ndoonjibaa.
Oodi-go keyaa North Bay, Ontario, Canada ingii-tazhi-nitaawig.[1]

I begin with this traditional Anishinaabe greeting to all my relatives in Creation. "Boozhoo indinawemaaganag" means "hello my relatives" in Anishinaabemowin (the Anishinaabe language). In the Anishinaabe cultural paradigm, our relatives have wings, fins, roots, paws, and hands; they are also made from liquid, air, rock, and fire. All of the beings in Creation know that they are supposed to take care of one another, for all parts of Creation are interconnected and dependent on one another to keep the balance of Aki (the earth). Our Inaakonigewin (laws) tell us that we are all related. These laws are what inform my knowledge, and I was taught to follow them by both my Elders and those cultural knowledge holders that have instructed me on how to live as an Anishinaabe-kwe (an Anishinaabe woman).

With this greeting, I seek to situate myself with the Anishinaabe-aki-ing (traditional territory) of my ancestors, both on Mishi-Mikinaakomi-nis (Turtle Island or North America) and on Ashkaakamigo-kwe (Mother Earth). Moreover, it prioritizes Indigeneity and establishes an Indigenized space for the Kwewag gikendaasowin miinwaa dibaajimowin (women's knowledge, teachings, and stories) that I share here through my words, thoughts, ideas, and theories. By sharing this greeting in both languages, I am reaching out to both Indigenous and non-Indigenous readers to feel welcome to learn about Anishinaabe-kwewag (women's) miinwaa Anishinaabe doodoom[2] (maternal, motherly) ecological knowledge, traditions, and worldviews but also to invite readers to share this knowledge as a way of educating others about Indigenous women's ways of knowing, doing, seeing, being, and relating to Aki.

I will be discussing Anishinaabe-kwewag maternal environmental activism in this chapter. This discussion includes examining the Anishinaabe worldview (ontology, epistemology, and axiology) held by leading Anishinaabe-kwewag maternal environmental activists, which will highlight the unique intersections between Anishinaabe cultural traditions relating to mothers, mothering, maternal philosophies of living, ecological advocacy, and environmental activism. Using examples of the Anishinaabe women activists who focus their advocacy on environmental issues related to Nibi (water)—including Winona LaDuke, Josephine Mandamin, Shirley Ida Williams, and Liz Osawamick— I will articulate their specific motivations and cultural contexts as maternal caregivers[3] in the pursuit of environmental activism and ecological advocacy. Highlighting these women's environmental activities will illustrate a framework of discourse on Anishinaabe sovereignty and self-representation that articulates a female-centred conceptualization of environmental activism through the lens of Indigeneity, maternal awareness, and ancient cultural and spiritual connections to the earth. By highlighting Indigenous maternal-based resistance to ecological colonization of the environment and traditional Indigenous territory, Anishinaabe mothers and grandmothers are demonstrating the necessity of Indigenous ways of living with the earth—that is, to be in right relations with other living beings and to have the strength to face powerful industrial realities using Indigenous ethics.

Indigenous maternal environmental activism within Anishinaabe-kwewag contexts is rooted in maternal identity, modes of resistance, cultural resurgence, ecological paradigms, and traditional cultural responsibilities as Kwewag[4] (women, females) in relation to Aki and Nibi. These components will often appear layered, stacked, interwoven, and often multidimensional in context. Furthermore, these components align with an Anishinaabe aaniin nayaanaagadawenamang (Anishinaabe philosophy), which contains Anishinaabe Ashkaakamigokwe Gikendaasowin (Anishinaabe Mother Earth–based knowledge). By prioritizing and privileging the Anishinaabe-kwewag worldview, I want to provide clarity and insight into the complexities of Anishinaabe-kwewag maternal environmental activists' motivations for resisting and challenging environmental threats to Indigenous sovereignty, health, and wellbeing. Additionally, representations of the Indigenous maternal environmental activism are lacking in the existing literature and need to be privileged in the scholarship to raise awareness and educate the public of the kinds of work Indigenous women are doing to protect and heal the environment as well as to sustain it for future generations. By highlighting the motivations, work, worldviews, discourse, and lived experiences of Anishinaabe-kwewag maternal environmental activists, we allow space for learning, dialogue, and growth as like-minded human beings concerned about the safety, longevity, and sustainability of Mother Earth.

The Worldview of Anishinaabe-kwewag Maternal Environmental Activists

In discussing and identifying Anishinaabe-kwewag maternal environmental activism, we must we must first contextualize the Anishinaabe-kwewag worldview concerning ecological and territorial understandings of relationality with Aki, which is the foundation of Indigenous identity and occupancy in North America. Anishinaabe Elder Onaubinisay James Dumont (Shawanaga First Nation) describes the Anishinaabe worldview as a 360-degree vision, meaning that Anishinaabe people are taught through our language and cultural practices to acknowledge the layers, levels, and multidimensions existent in all of Creation (Dumont 31-32). All of Creation includes the earth, the land, all the creatures that inhabit it, along with the air, sky, weather, stars, sun, moon, human beings, the Spirit realm(s), and so on. *Anishinaabe aaniin nayaanaagadawenamang* is the study of those general and fundamental questions concerning matters such as existence, knowledge, values, reason, the intellectual mind, and language. As Anishinaabe people, our cultural philosophy contains the intellectual traditions and information from generations of knowledge keepers. Our philosophies guide us to understand our relationship, roles, and responsibilities as human beings to everything in Creation. These intellectual understandings are rooted in our Anishinaabe wenji-ozhichigaadeg aki (cosmology), which includes our origin theories and the Gzhe-Manidoo Kiimiingona manda Gikendaasowin (The Creator's Original Instructions) that provide inaakonigewinan (laws) to uphold the earth's natural order. The *Gzhe*-Manidoo Kiimiingona manda Gikendaasowin informs human beings that before human Creation, all life on earth was given specific instructions to live and was instructed to share their knowledge with human beings on how to live following the natural order (Johnston, *Ojibway Heritage* 13; Geniusz 129). The original laws state how we are to act towards the land and other creatures that dwell on the earth. Furthermore, human beings were instructed that everything in Creation has a gift and knowledge through which human beings can learn to better live with the natural order. Gzhe-Manidoo gave us Anishinaabe aaniin ji-doodawangwaa giijininiwinaan miinwaa gikakiiminaan (values, morality, and ethics), which requires Anishinaabe people to stand up for the protection and sustainability of this storehouse of knowledge, life, and valuable resources necessary for human survival.

The Anishinaabe-kwewag maternal worldview is rooted in ensuring the sustainability of the land for our children and children's children. This worldview is also governed by our roles and responsibilities as the caregivers and caretakers of Ashkaakamigo-kwe's (Mother Earth's) children: those that grow from the land, those that fly, those that walk on four legs and two legs, and those beings that swim. The plants, animals, birds, fish, water, soil, and air that exist on earth are a part of what is called the Gzhe-Manidoo Ogitigan (Creator's garden) (Davidson-Hunt et al. 196). Anishinaabe people have a responsibility to the sustainability of the Creator's garden for both now, tomorrow, and for generations to come. Anishinaabe Elder Robin Greene (ban[5]) (Iskatewizaagegan/Shoal Lake First Nation) teaches that the Anishinaabe concept for sustainability is concerned with the custom of learning how to give back to Creation rather than taking (McGregor 72-91). Being a caretaker and a sustainability advocate is a sacred duty performed by both women and men, according to the teachings of the Gchi-Manidoo gaagige inaakonigewin (the Creator's great Eternal Laws of nature). This sacred duty places human beings as the *Gimiinigoowizimin Gaaganawendang* (caretakers, stewards, and protectors of the land) or the "Keepers of the Gifts" (Davidson-Hunt et al. 196). The Anishinaabe concept for sustainability requires human beings to act as advocates for the protection, renewal, and preservation of the gifts of Creation. Additionally, Elder Greene (ban) teaches that Gimiinigoowizimin Gaaganawendang speaks to "the gifts given for the *survival of the Anishinaabeg* as well as the moral responsibility the people bear to the Creator" (my emphasis, Davidson-Hunt et al. 196). In other words, we need nature not only to survive but, more importantly, to thrive. He explains further that Gimiinigoowizimin Gaaganawendang is an ethical and "moral, 'custodial' responsibility upon the Anishinaabe" (Davidson-Hunt et al. 196) to care for the earth as a relative. The principle of Gimiinigoowizimin Gaaganawendang supports a traditional Anishinaabe framework of ecological sustainability and active protection within an Anishinaabe paradigm and embedded within Anishinaabe Ashkaakamigo-kwe aaniin ji-doodawangwaa giijininiwinaan miiniwaa gikakiiminaan (earth-based morality and ethics). Moreover, to act sustainably as an Anishinaabe requires taking personal responsibility and becoming spiritually connected to all of Creation and time, including the past, present, and future. Maternal caregivers of Aki preserve our ancestor's legacy, ensure our children thrive, and safeguard resources for future generations; they act as guardians to offer security and insurance.

From this worldview, Anishinaabe women approach environmental advocacy and activism through unique ecological, ethnic, cultural, and gendered contexts and beliefs systems, which grounded in connections to the earth as Kwe (woman and female; and is inclusive of Two-Spirited people). We see our relationship as women to Mother Earth through our female-centred cultural teachings, which explain that as fellow women, mothers, and caregivers, we are connected to the female Spirit of the Great Mother Earth via our respective roles in the process of creating life, nurturing life, and sheltering new life from harm. We can find commonality with the earth as women and mothers because we work hard as mothers to provide for our children and use our body, mind, and spirit to nurture them. Even after the physical umbilical cord connecting the mother and child is cut, there remains a spiritual and emotional connection between the two. As our Creation stories tell us: human beings were created out of the raw elements of Mother Earth and set about on the land to evolve into present-day human beings, but we remain innately connected to the earth in much the same way a child does to its mother. This connection is born out of a necessity for survival. We as human beings must consume the earth's raw materials to nourish our bodies, shelter our bodies, and cloth our bodies; therefore, we continue to be dependent on her to live. However, our connections to the earth also arise from some deeper subconsciousness and spiritual need to connect with the land as a family.

The phrase "Akiing Gidisi'ewin" embodies this concept of an earth-based maternal connection. "Akiing" translates to "earth" or "territory," and Anishinaabe Darcy Ishpemingenzaabid Rheault translates "Gidisi'ewin" as "the navel way." She continues:

> It is the Mother connection. In the same way that my physical body was connected to my mother through my navel, my spirit is connected to *Eshkakimikwe*[6] through my spirit navel. But unlike the fact that my umbilical cord was cut at birth, my spiritual connection to *Eshkakimikwe* can never be severed. (97)

Akiing Gidisi'ewin is a key concept of the *Anishinaabe-kwewag* maternal ecological worldview because it prioritizes those ancient and abiding connections to traditional ancestral territory and relationality with the earth as woman, mother, and family.

As a scholar, mother, and Ojibwe/Nibiising Anishinaabe-kwe from a river island called Okikendawdt, and as a Ziibi Nibi-Ogitchidaakwe (a woman who protects the river water[7]), it is for me important to acknowledge the concepts that drive contemporary Anishinaabe maternal environmentalism because they drive my activism as both Kwe and doodoom to my nindaanis (daughters). Anishinaabe women work hard to make our communities stronger by ensuring the lands and waterways of our ancestors are viable spaces for our children now and for the future.

Colonizing the Water, Colonizing Kwe, Kwezens, and Two-Spirited People

I come from people who have lived next to lakes and rivers for generations upon generations. As an Anishinaabe-kwe, my ancestral territory stretches around much of the waterways of the northern Great Lakes region. The water of the rivers, lakes, rapids, waterfalls, springs, creeks, streams, ponds, and marshes in my territory are the foundation of my identity as an Anishinaabe-kwe doodoom (Anishinaabe mother). If I close my eyes and think of the French River, I can visualize every rock, overhanging tree, the best places to pull up a boat on certain islands so not to ruin a motor, and the best places to fish and pick berries. In a paper I wrote some time ago, I wrote the following:

> The waters of the French River and Dokis First Nation represent an intimate and critical aspect of my identity as an Anishinaabe-kwe. Without water and watersheds like the French River, Anishinaabeg individuals, like myself, would experience a fundamental disconnect with who we are as Anishinaabeg people. The water, along with the land, defines our identities, sustains our families and communities, and provides us with the knowledge of how to live as Anishinaabeg people. (91)

Today, these words loudly echo from my past as a tangible reminder that a disconnect is well underway between the water and the people. We still do not drink water straight from the lake, rivers, or streams on the French River or Lake Nipissing. If we do not do something to prevent the continued pollution of our waterways, ensure access to clean water for consumption by human beings and wildlife, and stop the exploitation of water resources, how can we continue to call ourselves Anishinaabe people or Gimiinigoowizimin Gaaganawendang? Our failure signifies we are not living up the original laws laid out for the Anishinaabe to follow. If human beings, animals, and plants have no clean water to consume, then the delicate natural connections that sustain the food chain and create the medicines required for survival will either be compromised irrevocably or will disappear entirely.

Fortunately, over the last decade, an Anishinaabe-kwewag maternal-based environmental movement has arisen. Anishinaabe mothers, grandmothers, Elders, maternal guardians, aunties, and Two-Spirited people are calling themselves Nibi-Ogitchidaakwewag (Water Protectors or Those Women Who Defend the Water) or also Nibi-Mide-Ogichidaakwewag (Medicine Warriors for the Spirit of the Water). As Water Protectors and Water Warriors, our responsibility is safeguarding water because of the fundamental belief that Bimaadiziwin Nibi Aawan! (Water Is Life!). Our voice, our purpose in life, and our power as women, girls, and Two-Spirited people lie with the water. Anishinaabe women carry the water in our bodies; we pray and sing to the water in our ceremonies and ceremonial lodges. Anishinaabe women, girls, and Two-Spirited people are called "Keepers of the Water" or 'Carriers of the Water' during our ceremonies. These are our women's teachings, which embody the sacred connections females have to the water in our bodies. Water represents many aspects of a Kwe's life, including such emotional responses as crying, the health of our cells, food digestion, menstruation cycles, fertility, pregnancy, births, breastfeeding, and menopause. Directing a woman's life is the relationship she has with the water she holds in her body and the water that comes to her from the earth. Water is essential to all Indigenous women as illustrated by the words of Stoh:Loh writer Lee Maracle (Tsleil-Waututh First Nation):

I am familiar with the water in my body. My eyes have shed tears, drop by drop; my womb has gushed a torrent of water prior to the birth of each of my children. I have bled drops of blood, month by month, as a woman. I understand water and how each drop is so hard won; each drop is so fought for, so essential to my being. Without it, I am dead. Without it, I am a wrinkled old prune, an empty shell. (34).

In all of Creation, water is the great sustainer, and even Mother Earth requires her to survive. The cycles of the water through, over, and under the earth are a powerful dance that keeps us all alive. Nlaka'pamux scholar Ardith Wal'petko We'dalx Walkem (Nlaka'pamux First Nation) writes:

> Water teaches us that everything is cyclical. Living without regard for the cyclical nature of water has resulted in newcomer society acting as though there are no repercussions to logging watersheds, releasing pollutants and other contaminants into water, or consuming water for industrial, agricultural, or domestic purposes beyond viable levels. (310)

However, over generations, Indigenous women's bodies, territorial rights, and connection to the water have experienced colonization at the hands of non-Indigenous nations and cultures. Likewise, water itself has also endured colonization. The colonization of water comes from the occupation and desecration of the land, animals, birds, plants, trees, and waterways. Additionally, the colonization of water is evident in the elimination of Indigenous women, girls, and Two-Spirited people from their territories due to treaties, forced relocations, the Indian Act, the residential school system, the Sixties Scoop, incarceration, urbanization, unemployment, poverty, and the foster care system. Furthermore, Indigenous women, girls, and Two-Spirited people have experienced the erosion of their covenant with water, particularly to our lakes, rivers, springs, and streams, along with our bodies, and also our cultural traditions related to water. The Indian Act banned Indigenous water ceremonies, such as the Cree Sundance or Thirst Dance, but also caused the diminished practice of other Indigenous water ceremonies on the threat of jail. Indigenous fasting, sweat lodge ceremonies, birth ceremonies, death ceremonies, and puberty rites were all outlawed by the Canadian government and religious Christian leaders that managed the reserve system. Colonial policies disrupted Indigenous women, girls, and Two-Spirited people's abilities to build healthy relationships with water, to learn protocols and procedures of honouring water, and to perform the ceremonies of gratitude for the water. For a long time, Anishinaabe women, girls, and Two-Spirited people practiced in secret or did not perform the birth ceremonies, puberty rites, prayers, and the songs to the water.

The colonization of water is one of the most significant threats to Indigenous sovereignty and survival ever faced by the Indigenous population of Turtle Island:

> The slaughter of the animals and the destruction of the *water* led to the starvation of my people and the disconnection from all that empowered us. If someone had said to my ancestors that you could destroy the waters, they would likely have laughed - it turns out that this is in the realm of the possible. The *waters* of Snauq'w are gone. Housing, docks, businesses, apartments, roads, and the railway station have replaced it, and the garden that Snauq'w was is now destroyed. There is no shoreline left, so the plants that sustained the life of the *water* are gone as well. There are thousands of people living on top of the destroyed *water*. This destruction severely weakened all Salish people, and it surely rendered the *water* impotent. (my emphasis, Maracle 35)

Maracle acknowledges that before there was a Canada, her people were able to care for one another and to share the bounty harvested and hunted from the land; they never had to wonder if there would be food or water left for future generations (Maracle 35). She states that now "Canada is a guest who moved into our house, tossed us out, and then destroyed everything in the house" (35).

The real question here is how are we going to recreate a society in which our women can be sovereign, healthy, and Anishinaabe-kwe? According to the teachings of Mohawk midwife and Elder Katsi Cook, the first environment is the starting place for it all and the best indicator of how or why to proceed. Cook, as a midwife, believes everything the mother feels, eats, and sees affects the baby. That is part of her belief system. Therefore, if you want to find a reason to save the water, it means you are also protecting the nation because women birth the nation. Without the life sustaining properties of water, women will not be able to provide for their children. In effect, by colonizing the water and the women, the entire nation breaks down and the original covenant with water is jeopardized. It is for this reason, that environmental, maternal-based resistance to further colonization of the water is an urgent mission for Anishinaabe mothers and grandmothers across Anishinaabe-akiing. As Anishinaabe midwife Carol Couchie explains, "Nishnawbe women are the guardians of their culture, families and communities.... This is the very future of our Nations" (Couchie and Nabigon 49). It is time for Anishinaabe women to remember their covenant with the water and that they are Gimiinigoowizimin Gaaganawendang.

Nibi Is a Treaty

"Waawiindaganeziwin" translates to "words are treaties," which is how I have learned to understand my relationship with Nibi (water) as an Anishinaabe-kwe. Nibi acts as a critical reminder of the covenant or treaty between human beings and the Spirit of the water. Indigenous treaty making is an ancient process created for the mutual benefit of nations for the shared use of territory, people, and resources within the natural order devised by the Gzhe-Manidoo. When a mother gives birth and begins building a relationship with her child, she goes about showing and telling the child how to treat her while simultaneously learning the child's needs. The child learns not to abuse its mother's body or her resources, and the mother learns to provide selflessly and to not deny the necessities of life, such as breastmilk, clothing, shelter, and love. Motherhood and childhood, such as treaty making, is about balance and relationship building. As Michi Saagig Nishnaabeg scholar Leanne Betasamosake Simpson writes:

> When my second child *Minowewebeneshiinh* came into our lives, she brought with her a deeper understanding of these teachings [on treaties]. She taught me about balance—that if relationships get out of balance, then that imbalance can affect the health and wellness of the mama and the baby. She taught me that those early years set the tone for the entire relationship. That's why that time is so important and we have to be so careful and so gentle with our children. *Minowewe* taught me that both the mother and the child have to be taken care of, in order for the relationship to work. So in treaties, the relationship must be one of balance. One nation cannot be dominant over the other. One nation cannot control all of the land and all of the resources. (my emphasis, Simpson 107).

Balance, moderation, self-control, and maintaining a healthy relationship comes first above all else in the treaty process.

Upholding, maintaining, and fostering treaty relationships with the water speaks to a kind of stewardship bound within traditional legal responsibilities, which is known as bimeekumaugaewin—a mechanism of enforcement for upholding treaty laws (Borrows 80). The first law of bimeekumaugaewin involves the enforcement of gaamiinigooyang (Borrows 79), which acknowledges that the water (or some other living thing, such as trees, air, and soil) is alive and put on earth by the Creator for a higher purpose to fulfill. All Indigenous peoples across Turtle Island have similar laws with regards to water, as Maracle asserts:

> We do not own the water, the *water owns itself*. We are responsible for ensuring that we do not damage the water. We do not have an absolute right to use and abuse the water; we must take care of the water and ensure that we have a good relationship with it. This relationship is based on mutual respect. (my emphasis, Maracle 37)

The second law of bimeekumaugaewin is gikinoo'amaadiwin, which stipulates that it is up to human beings to not interfere with the natural order and allow the gikinoo'amaadiwin (Creator's vision) to unfold and to let the motion of life continue (Borrows 79). Finally, the treaty also requires gwayakochigewin or accountability, which necessitates that human beings be responsible for their choices, actions, and outcomes (Borrows 79). The principles of Bimeekumaugaewin must cycle into one another to achieve harmony. Currently, throughout Anishinaabe-akiing, water is threatened, sick, and dying. Failure to act will result in disapprobation (tubuhumahgawin) or failure to meet treaty responsibilities (Borrows 80). All life needs water to survive; therefore, it is critical to maintain the functioning of the cycle of water's bimeekumaugaewin.

Among the Anishinaabe, a treaty with water requires human beings to put the wellbeing of the water before human self-interest. Placing water first also means placing water's dependents first, including the rights of animals, birds, and plants, which require water from Mother Earth to live. Treaty making with water also includes reaffirmation ceremonies, such as the repetitive offering of semaa (tobacco) or kinnikinnick (plant medicine mixture), anamewinan (prayers), and nagamonan (songs) to the water, Mother Earth, and the Creator as signs of gratitude and goodwill. Conducting these actions would allow human beings to survive and to instinctively know how to live in harmony and balance with all Creation.

What drives Anishinaabe-kwewag as maternal environmental activists to act for the sake of water? It begins specifically with human beings' ancient treaty with water. Furthermore, it is defined and predicated upon the Gzhe-Manidoo Kiimiingona manda Kendaaswin (The Creator's Original Instructions) and the Gchi-Manidoo gaagige inaakonigewin (Creator's Sacred and Eternal Laws) embedded inside the instructions. It is these laws that instruct and detail the responsibilities of Anishinaabe women to honour, protect, and heal the water. At the time of human Creation, everything on earth agreed to a covenant with the Creator to facilitate the survival of human beings, including the water (Johnston, *Ojibway Heritage* 16, 49-50). Water agreed to nourish and cleanse us, but in return, human beings had to uphold the sovereignty of water and respect the many treaties water had with all the other creatures living on the land, water, air, and sky. The human treaty with the water prioritizes principles of noninterference, which mean that a human being will never interfere in any way with the rights, privileges, and activities of water or with any other living creature's access to or use of water. Every living creature on Turtle Island—including the muskrat, loon, dragonfly, snake, fish, bird, worm, and frog—needs water to survive. And water requires its independence, sovereignty, and respect from other living beings. Maracle declares the following: "I will always want sovereignty. *Like the water,* I will never give it up.... The water belongs to everyone. The water belongs to itself. We are responsible for taking care of it. In exchange we get to use it—sparingly. In the Salish tradition, we have an obligation to the water" (my emphasis, Maracle 37).

For Anishinaabe children, Nibi is the very first treaty relationship they will enter into in their life. Before we are even born into this world, we form a treaty relationship with water and inherit the covenant our ancestors formed with the water at the time of human creation. The brain and heart are composed of 73 per cent water, and the lungs are about 83% water. The skin contains 64% water, muscles and kidneys are 79 per cent water; even the bones are watery, 31 per cent (Mitchell et al. 628, 630). Each day, humans need to consume a certain amount of water to survive; therefore, a human being's treaty relationship with water is of paramount significance.

Beginning when we are just babies, Anishinaabe females are trained to respect, understand, and enact this treaty relationship. Girls hear and are then taught the words to water songs; they carry the water into ceremonies and learn about their treaty responsibilities. As we grow older and become more aware of our reproductive roles within our families, communities, and nation, girls, youth, and women will learn about the role water has in their fertility journey. Oral stories provide teachings to young girls and youth about how life begins with water, how to care for the water in our bodies, and how to use that water to create life through our bodies. These young women learn the cultural knowledge and science of how water is vital to life giving. For instance, water is in the follicular fluid that surrounds the giwaawan (ripening ovum) on the waawaniwazh (ovary). The gaa-izhibiindenig abinoojiizhens onibiim jibwaa-nitaawigid (amniotic sac) is filled with abinoojiizhens onibiim (amniotic fluid or sometimes called mide-waaboo, which means medicine water). Abinoojiizhens onibiim (amniotic fluid) is the home of the gigishkawaawaswaan (unborn fetus) for nine months and contains vital fats, proteins, electrolytes, and carbohydrates, which are necessary for ensuring health, wellbeing, and proper development ("Pregnancy Amniotic Fluid"). In her ipay (uterus), the Anishinaabe mother shares her vital gimiskwiim (lifeblood) to her child through the dabinoojiizhensim odapikweshimon (placenta) and then through the *gidisi'ewin* (umbilical cord or "The navel way. Mother connection in you" [Rheault xxiv]). While in the womb, the fetus develops its waawaniwazhan (ovaries); therefore, the mother's water begins nurturing both the fetus and her future grandchildren. Upon birth, water breaks forth and cleanses the way for the baby to exist the onji-bimi-nitaawigid giniijaanis (birth canal). After birth, the mother reaffirms the treaty with the water when she brings the baby to her breast to get its first feeding of breastmilk (doodooshaaboo). Finally, the baby is given its first bath in water or cedar water, which ratifies the treaty relationship with water.[8]

I understand the treaty with water as the first treaty I introduced my daughters to as infants. In my family, Indigenous maternal environmental activism began when I was in my mother's womb because I carried the ovaries that would be used to grow my daughters. When my daughters were just mere ovaries in my body, they were already initiating their treaty responsibilities to Nibi and Aki. I breastfed my girls sitting in front of the river waters of the French River and bathed them in the river waters; "Nibi" was the first Ojibwe word I taught my daughters speak. Providing their education as Water Carriers and Keepers of the Water is a tremendous responsibility, but that is what it truly means to be an Anishinaabe-kwe and doodoom. Such preparation deserves respect and honour; therefore, my daughters will learn the covenant they joined long before they were born; they will learn the words, the songs, and songs of the "Carriers of the Sacred Water." Our treaty relationship as women, mothers, and grandmothers is centred in water and extends outwards through our daughters and granddaughters to Gii'kinaaganaa (all our relations/all our relatives): our families, communities, nations, and the natural world.

Nibi-Ogitchidaa-Kwewag: Those Women Who Defend the Water

The teachings of the lifeway of the Anishinaabe, called the Anishinaabe Mino-Miikana Bimaadiziwin, are a significant directive, which guides the work of the women who protect the water through environmental activism. "Anishinaabe Mino-Miikana Bimaadiziwin" translates to "the good way of living that all Anishinaabe women and men should follow in order to find health and wellbeing in life." If we follow the knowledge and ethics encoded in our traditional teachings, we will then fulfill our purpose as human beings and find peace, balance, and harmony with the natural world, as the Creator intended it to be. The purpose of all Anishinaabe people is to stay true to the Mino-Miikana Bimaadiziwin (the good lifeway, the good path of life, or the good road of life). If we lose our way from the path, we know that we can always find our way back to the Mino-Miikana.

According to Anishinaabe environmentalist Winona LaDuke, "There is no way to quantify a way of life, only a way to live it. "Minobimaatisiiwin" means 'the good life.' Used in blessings, thanksgivings, and ceremonies, it refers to the *lifeway*" (my emphasis, LaDuke "All Our Relations" 132). Anishinaabe Elder James Dumont argues something similar:

> Our ways are still there, our way of life.... we say the reality that we live within is totally different from anything we say the reality that we live within is totally different from anything we ever knew. It is just a different environment, a different context. Not a very good one, not a very harmonious or balanced one, not a very healthy one, but this is the environment that we live in today. The *lifeway* that spoke to our people before, and gave our

people life that will give us life today. How it will manifest itself and find expression in this new time comes as a part of the responsibility of how we go about the revival and renewal. (my emphasis, Thorpe 79)

The lifeways of Indigenous women maternal caregivers—including mothers, grandmothers, guardians, aunties, and so on—have been compromised by colonization. Policies aggressively targeted women's cultures, bodies, minds, spirits, territories, and knowledge systems focused on preventing women from contributing to the growth of Indigenous nations, rights, and freedoms. However, since the introduction of colonial legal traditions and these policies of assimilation, Anishinaabe women have also worked to counter, undermine, and challenge any threat to their sovereignty and cultural lifeways. Evidence of these strategies of survival arise in the Anishinaabe-kwewag maternal environmental activism, which is related to the protection of the integrity and purity of water from pollution, extraction, and so on.

Since the 1980s, Anishinaabe women have politically asserted their cultural roles as Water Carriers and Keepers of the Water, and publically began referring to themselves as Water Protectors ("Liz Oswamick Shares her Water Song with the Roberston Program"). Some Anishinaabe Water Protectors do not like to be referred to as activists, environmentalists, or protestors; instead, they try to frame the context for their work within traditional terminology or just acting as good citizens of their nations. Indigenous women's environmentalism-based resistance and public awareness campaigns have had significant impacts on environmental activism throughout Canada and the United States by shaping discourse, methods, and mediums of resistance. These women have taken their voices and knowledge to the general public, engaging with environ-mentalism at public lectures, conferences, symposiums, and political events. Furthermore, these women are informing environmentalists of the challenges faced by Indigenous peoples and Indigenous territories while also rallying allies and aid for their radical resistance projects. Indigenous women began a relationship with environmental activism because it was a venue for public recognition and empowerment against the political and economic forces in North American society that threaten Indigenous survival. For this reason, Indigenous women, mothers, and grandmothers realized the need to develop Anishinaabe resistance discourses, definitions, and activities rooted in Anishinaabe-based environmental activism as a means to advocate for the protection, longevity, and, ultimately, the sustainability of Indigenous territory for current and future generations. Anishinaabe women have been some of the most well-known national and international environmentalists and environmental activists in North America.

The following are a few leading Anishinaabe-kwewag maternal environmental activists: Winona LaDuke, Josephine Mandamin, Shirley Williams, and Elizabeth (Liz) Osawamick. They represent just some of the women who are shaping the resurgence of Kwewag sovereignty and the sovereignty of both Nibi and Aki.

Winona LaDuke: "I am Anishinaabe, and I Am a Water Protector!" ("Winona LaDuke Address Fargo—We Are Water Protectors)

One of the most well-known Anishinaabe women activists is Winona LaDuke (Gaawaabaabanikaag, White Earth Reservation). Along with being a worldwide-known Indigenous environmentalist, LaDuke is also a mother, a grandmother, a scholar, an economist, a farmer, and a political speaker. Since the 1980s, LaDuke has been working to protect the land and water of Anishinaabe-akiing. She has worked to define Indigenous- and Anishinaabe-specific environmental sustainability while promoting tribal relocalization, defaming multinational corporations, and overthrowing what she refers to as "Windigo economics"[9] ("Winona LaDuke—Honor the Earth"). In our oral traditions, Windigoes are cannibalistic, demonlike creatures that have an insatiable hunger and will kill anything and anyone to feed its appetite. Scholar Basil Johnston (ban) says that the Windigoes are a good representation of modern Western's society's hunger for resources (Johnston, *The Manitous* 233-35). The *Windigoes* have moved among us disguised in various new forms and taken residence in politics, economics, culture, and society. They can found in the disparities in the economic distribution of wealth as well as in the political paradigms that deem some people food and fodder for others. Next, they are part of the ravenous and unconscionable extraction of the earth's resources (rock, soil, gems, oil, and so on). They arise in the industrial development and technological investments that poison and kill the land and water, and are also found in the individualistic social structures that focus on the now, not the future. These are the contemporary footprints of the Windigo economics referred to by LaDuke.

LaDuke is a herald, a trickster, and a warrior for the Indigenous community against the modern-day dangers that the Windigoes represent. Long ago, the Nibiising Anishinaabe were terrorized by Windigoes at Lake Nipissing in the area of what is now Nipissing First Nation (Johnston, *The Manitous* 233-35). The people called for Nanaboozho, and he came to defend them, luring the *Windigoes* from the hilltop and out into Lake Nipissing to drown them. He outsmarted the Windigoes and today, LaDuke is there to outsmart, outlast, and defend the Anishinaabe people, along with any Indigenous people that call her to their side as the Anishinaabe did with Nanaboozho. One of the focuses of her environmentalism is Indigenous water sovereignty.

At a recent conference on March 10, 2018, held at the University of Washington, she said, "I am a Water Protector" ("Winona LaDuke—Honor the Earth). Underlying much of LaDuke's work is the traditional teachings of the Anishinaabe Seven Fires Prophecy, which explains that the Anishinaabe people are living through an age that asks them to choose whether to continue treading on "the scorched path: they have pursued thus far or, conversely, to choose "the green path" (Benton-Banai 89-93). LaDuke explains the following:

We are in a moment. It is prophesied in our time and it is referred to as the time of the seventh fire. We are told as Anishinaabeg people that we have a choice between two paths. One path they say is well worn and it is scorched. The other path is not well worn and it is green. We are told that it is our choice on which path to embark. I am really sure that is where we all are at this moment. As you look out there in the final stages of the fossil fuel economy and the thrashing of an inefficient economy, which I refer to it as a *Windigo economy*, it is in its final stages of that life where it is running out of things to dig out of the earth and running out of oil and extreme opportunities. They have become so aggressive in their final hours. It is really incumbent upon us to summon every bit of courage to stand against them and to move to the next economy. So that is what this is about, that moment. (my emphasis, "Winona LaDuke—Honor the Earth")

For LaDuke, the "green path" is a postpetroleum, land-based economy, which moves away from fossil fuels and plastic; instead, it focuses on a balanced and harmonious intergenerational and interspecies coexistence on Mother Earth. If Anishinaabe people are to survive, LaDuke advocates an "elegant transition" ("Seventh Annual Judith Davidson Moyers Women of Spirit Lecture") out of the Windigo economies dependent on fossil fuels and into economies of self-sufficiency and self-determination. "We Anishinaabe people have a word for the process of determining our destiny: *Ji misawaabandaaming*. This process is essential for our survival as Indigenous peoples," explains LaDuke ("Anishinaabe Prophecy"). She suggests that to achieve sovereignty and self-determination, Anishinaabe people must address how we use our environment, how we allow others to use our territories, an how we address the viabilities of our current economic existence in order to plot a path for our future economies. She explains to the *Anishinaabe* people and other Indigenous peoples across North America that "In this millennium, we must undergo a conscious transformation and take technological and economic leaps to develop tribal energy and food security" ("Anishinaabe Prophecy"). LaDuke argues that for contemporary Indigenous people, communities, and nations that water is more important than oil: "We love our land and our water. We all have a covenant with the Creator to take of that which the Creator gave us" ("Winona LaDuke").

LaDuke recently described herself as a Water Protector and shared the story of how she returned sturgeon to Round Lake on Gaawaabaabanikaag-akiing for her family, her people, and all her relatives in Creation (LaDuke "Anishinaabe Prophecy"). In this story, she went to Rainy River First Nation for a powwow and met Al Hunter and his brother Joe Hunter who both run a hatchery for sturgeon. Interested in getting some sturgeon to reintroduce to the waterways on Gaawaabaabanikaag-akiing she returned a week later and collected five four-year-old fish. After successfully crossing the Canadian-American border, LaDuke put her sturgeon into Round Lake. The sturgeon thrived and repopulated the waters of Gaawaabaabanikaag-akiing. LaDuke takes pride in the fact that she kept her covenant with the water and also that she rekindled her relationship with the sturgeon. As a Kwe, doodoom, and nookomis (grandmother), LaDuke fulfilled her responsibilities as a Gimiinigoowizimin Gaaganawendang. The reintroduction of the sturgeon began the water's healing process on Gaawaabaabanikaag-akiing, and the act is also a reaffirmation of her community's covenant between human beings and the water. To this, she shares:

> When my first grandson was born, his clan was sturgeon clan. I was very proud to say, *"My grandson, look what Grannie got you!"* I say that because we are related to those fish, and those fish are our relatives: *indinawemaaganag.* Those are our relatives. So to me, *Name,* the sturgeon, this is what a *Water Protector* looks like. As mighty as they can be, as old as they can be, and a regal as they can be. I tell those Enbrige Gas guys that I do not do this work for you to pollute our waters. We brought our relatives home! (LaDuke "Anishinaabe Prophecy")

Rooted in prophecy, LaDuke's maternal-based environmental activism and advocacy are concerned about the choice between two paths—"one green and lush, the other well-worn but scorched"—for which she clearly sees that as women, mothers, and grandmothers, "We are not just fighting against something, but clearly and decidedly walking with open eyes and hearts down the path that is green" (qtd. in Bellow). As LaDuke explains, if the Earth is taken from us, if it is damaged or its resources are pillaged and abused, like the water, then we will have nothing left, and we may cease to be Anishinaabe:

> The struggle of Indigenous peoples to protect our mother earth is a struggle that continues; it is unrelenting because she is the only mother we know. We have no place to go from our territories, and our very existence is contingent upon the protection and the relationship we have with our mother earth. (Seventh Annual Judith Davidson Moyers Women of Spirit Lecture)

The Water Walkers

Like LaDuke, other Anishinaabe women have become leaders in the fight for environmental justice relating to water. "It's all about the water. It's not about me. It's not about the walkers. It's about the water" ("Anishinaabe Water Walkers Trek), states Anishinaabe Elder Josephine Mandamin (*Wikwemikong* Unceded First Nation) about the Water Walker movement she helped to establish in 2003. In the 1990s, Elder Mandamin began raising awareness of the poor state of water in

First Nations communities and she started ceremonial walks for the water, walking with a copper pail[10] full of water in one hand and a staff in the other ("Meet Josephine Mandamin"). Her message to the world has always been this: "The water of Mother Earth, she carries life to us, and as women we carry life through our bodies. We as women are life-givers, protectors of the water, and that's why we are very inclined to give mother earth the respect that she needs for the water" ("Meet Josephine Mandamin").

In 2000, a prophecy from an Elder within the Three Fires Midewiwin Society was presented to Elder Mandamin, and it warned that "water will cost as much as gold" by the year 2030 ("Grandmother Josephine Mandamin"). She notes that the Elder asked her what she was going to do about it all, and her answer was to not just talk about doing something but to "Walk the Talk" ("Meet Josephine Mandamin"). By 2003, she had grown concerned over the unhealthy state of the waters of the Great Lakes region of Ontario. Elder Mandamin desired to raise awareness of water pollution and its impact on Indigenous people, which led her to organize ceremonial walks over thousands of kilometres along the shorelines of many of the Great Lakes and river ways to demonstrate the importance of protecting water resources ("Trekking the Great Lakes on Foot"). Mandamin notes that she grew up eating fish and drinking water straight from Georgian Bay, but over the years, she has witnessed the waters become polluted, rendering it undrinkable, and the water tables lowering due to climate change, which is alarming since the Great Lakes "provide drinking water to 35 million people" (McMahon). As a mother and grandmother, Elder Mandamin saw the bleak future Indigenous people if she did not act to make change for the better.

In 2003, Elder Mandamin chose to dedicate the rest of her life to not only acknowledging that the water is sacred but getting others to recognize that reality. She did this by walking the perimeter of every Great Lake on both sides of the shared Canadian and American border with a band of supporters called the Mother Earth Water Walkers. To the mothers and grandmothers whose responsibility it is to protect the water, Elder Mandamin's call to action message is clear:

We really need to think as women, as life-givers that we understand the meaning of the water and how it gives life just the way women give life. We honour our mother the earth as a life-giver to and we really need to take care of her, the way she has taken care of us. No, she is having a lot of turmoil, going through a lot of pain, and unable to feed her children in other parts of the world. She is really suffering, she is really crying out for us to help her. She has helped us all these years, all these hundreds of millions of years. She has been beautifully giving us part of her life, her water and now it is our turn to take care of her. We need to really fight for her, so that she can be forever giving us her water; especially, for those next generations to come, yet to come. They will need the water to nourish them and keep them healthy. ("Nokomis Josephine Mandamin")

Mandamins's call to action caused many mother and grandmothers to join her Water Walks or to organize walks in their territories.

From 2010 to 2018, following Mandamin's call to action, Elder Shirley Ida Williams and Elizabeth (Liz) Osawamick organized annual water walks around the Kawartha Lakes region of Ontario, called the Nibi Emosaawdamajig (Those Who Walk for the Water) (Johnson, "It's Really Very Crucial Right Now"; Kapyrka). Williams and Osawamick's primary concern was to raise awareness of the dozens of First Nation communities constantly under boil water advisories. According to the CBC News, "Two thirds of First Nations communities in Canada have experienced boil water advisories in the last 10 years" (Johnson, "It's Really Very Crucial Right Now"). Seeking to highlight the land and water where they currently live, the women have chosen to conduct walks at the water of Odoonabii-ziibi (Otonabee River in Peterborough) or the "river that beats like a heart."

Elder Williams believes that water is life. She teaches the importance of walking for water awareness: "It's really very crucial right now because a lot of communities can't drink the water. A lot of First Nations communities cannot drink the water because it's become poison" (qtd. in Johnson, "'It's Really Very Crucial Right Now"). Furthermore, she advocates that everyone makes it a priority to become educated about the state of the water in their territories and communities as well as to join together for the future of clean water in Canada before it is too late. "We're coming together to make awareness to take care of the water. Regardless if you're an Aboriginal person or not, we need to work together to keep the waters clean" (Johnson "It's Really Very Crucial Right Now'").Elder Williams is proud of the fact that women are taking up the cause of clean water and working to find ways to protect the water, such as the yearly water walks: "I have seen women change how they look at the water, how they treat the water. They make changes within themselves and also within their family. They stop putting chemicals in the water. They'll save water" (qtd. in Vasil). Elder Williams extends Elder Mandamin's calls for the women to "take up the call to bring local awareness to our communities about the sacredness of Nibi and the perils that face the waterways in our homelands" (Williams).

As spiritual leaders in the community, many people listen to the words and follow the actions of Elders Mandamin and Williams. They both have walked many times for the sake of the water, demonstrating that Anishinaabe-kwewag spiritual connections are grounded in ceremonies of reaffirmation, ceremony, but never protest. Anishinaabe-kwewag maternal environmental activism is about the resurgence and reeducation of our women to remember the land as our Mother, as we are mothers. She explains that "In our ceremonies it is the woman who will bless the water because women are the carriers of the water" ("Liz Osawamick: Need to Get Back to the Old Ways"). Just as water is the lifeblood of Mother Earth, water is the lifeblood of the unborn children mothers carry in their wombs. Elder Williams adds that "We carry babies in our wombs and it's the water that comes out first." "In the ceremony," she continues, "there will be water carried in a copper pail" to represent our female—*Kwe*—responsibilities as givers of life, just as Mother Earth gives us, her children, life (qtd. in Johnson "It's Really Very Crucial Right Now"). Without Mother Earth and her water, life would wither and die.

Both Elder Williams and her niece Liz Osawamick have discussed how passionate they are for doing the walks for the water. Like so many of the communities that still have no access to clean drinking water, Liz Oswamick recalls memories from her childhood when access to clean water was a precious commodity for her family ("Liz Osawamick: Need to Get Back to the Old Ways"). She speaks about her beliefs in the sacredness of water because not everyone has access to it or has to work hard to get it. Oswamick explains that in her family, water was life, food, and medicine:

Yesterday when I was sharing about carrying that water because we didn't have water, we didn't have plumbing growing up, and having to walk a mile to get the water. Going back to that, I think of my father who planted, and we had a garden every year. I remember that he would always collect the rainwater. He would have those barrels of rainwater to use to plant and water his garden. It is those kinds of things that we need to go back to. Just those little things, such as saving that rainwater. To protect our medicines, our plants, and our trees. ("Liz Osawamick: Need to Get Back to the Old Ways")

To Oswamick, water is sacred, and it is crucial for women to get out and advocate for it. She charges that "We are made of water [and] it's [critical] that they know how sacred and important the water is to everyone" (qtd. in Vasil). She further teaches the following:

We as Anishinaabe believe that the Earth is like our mother. From her, we have everything that sustains us.... The water is like her lifeblood. All the bodies of water are her veins. Without water, we would not be here. It's so important that we educate the people about the importance of how sacred the water is. (qtd. in Johnson "It's Really Very Crucial Right Now")

Her purpose in walking to acknowledge the sacredness of water also extends to her walking to educate young people and rally the youth to reaffirm their ecological connections to ancestral territory: "We do it for seven generations and beyond. We have to start praying and talking to the water. We have to make sure that our kids understand that" ("Liz Oswamick Shares Her Water Song").

Oswamick states that she feels that mothers and grandmothers have the duty to initiate the connection that younger generations can have with water so that they can become protectors and sustainers rather than takers, abusers, and consumers ("Liz Oswamick shares her Water Song"). She offers a prayerful song of thanks to the water called *Nibi Nagamowin* (The Water Song). The song is also her call to the mothers and grandmothers to rise and become Water Protectors. The prayer goes as follows:

Nibi, Gizaagi'igo.
Water, we love you.

Gimiigwechiwenimigo.
We thank you.

Gizhawenimigo.
We respect you; we have compassion for you.

Ho! ("Liz Oswamick shares her Water Song")

As these Anishinaabe women demonstrate, maternal environmental activism is rooted in complex reasons of survival, sustainability, cultural resurgence as Indigenous nations, and understandings of our role in the order of Creation. Anishinaabe mothers and grandmothers are fighting for the land to protect those resources for our children and the survival of future generations. More than that, these women are also trying to preserve women's cultural and spiritual traditions. They resist the colonization of our waterways not only to uphold the cultural and legal sovereign rights of the natural world but also to assert the rights of Mother Earth as a living being of Spirit and consciousness. As Maracle warns, "The water owns itself," and we must not seek to favour our rights over that of the water (Maracle 38). She further notes the following:

> To entitle ourselves to own the water is to put ourselves ahead of it, in front of it, and on top of it—that is invasion. We are entitled to overuse what we own, to destroy what we own—burn it should we choose—but if we don't own it, then we can only engage it in relationship. We have to seek permission from it and to use it. We must care for it. (Maracle 38)

As women and as human beings, we have to let the water be our teacher because she embodies the Gagige Inaakonige (Eternal Laws) of the Creator inside her essence. Women were given the job of speaking and protecting the water because of its life-giving qualities match our own and guide our lives on earth, so it is time we all take up the responsibility of protecting water as *Kwewag*.

From Anishinaabe Elder Mahngese Herb Nabigon (ban) from Pic River First Nation, I learned to call the water my sister. Nibi, Elder Nabigon says, is called Sister-Water or Older-Sister-Water, which in Anishinaabemowin is Nimisenh Nibi (Nabigon 112). Now is the time to protect our big sister because for generations upon generations she has protected us, cared for us, healed us, nourished us, and cleansed us. I have two older sisters, and every time I think of all they have given to me, taught me, and sacrificed for me, I can feel great love for water as

Older-Sister-Water. Miigwech gaaye Nimisenh Nibi for teaching me about relationships, motherhood, and womanhood.

"We Will Go to Any Lengths for the Water": Concluding Thoughts

I thought I would finish this chapter with something that honours Aki, the Earth as Mother, Nibi the Spirit of water, and Kwewag, the carriers, keepers, and protectors of the water. The song below is an Anishinaabe/Algonquin Water Song. This song is sung to the water to speak to the Spirit of the water and communicate that we remember our responsibilities to it as an inawemaagan (a relative). For a very long time, these songs were only sung by our women in secret, in ceremonies, and only among those who could remember, but it is now time that all hear this song and others like them. The songs have the power and agency that our women are seeking to establish nationally and internationally. Everyone needs to listen to the songs of the water and remember the importance water has in our life. Furthermore, it is time for human beings to remember all the different songs dedicated to the water, to start singing them in their respective languages, and to sing them on their territories. Indigenous maternal environmental activism is not merely a protest walk or a speech; it is also expressed in sacred songs. Anishinaabe Nibi Waaboo goes as follows:

Nibi waaboo endaayang, aki miskwi nibi waaboo
Hey ya, hey ya, hey ya, hey
Hey ya, hey ya, hey ya, ho

Nibi waaboo endaayang, aki miskwi nibi waaboo
Hey ya, hey ya, hey ya, hey
Hey ya, hey ya, hey ya, ho

Nibi waaboo endaayang, aki miskwi nibi waaboo
Hey ya, hey ya, hey ya, hey
Hey ya, hey ya, hey ya, ho

Miigwech, Nii'kinaaganaa!

Endnotes

1. Greetings to all my relatives, all my relations. My traditional Spirit name is Woman-Who-Paints-Like-the-Sky. I am an Ojibwe (Those Who Keep Records of a Vision) and Nipissing Anishinaabe woman. I am Marten clan. I come from over there, across the lake by the "Place where the waters flow from the East" on the "Island of the Kettle Pots" (Dokis First Nation) and also by those "at the little water." I currently live in North Bay, Ontario, Canada

2. Doodoom is a singular term for mother, and doodooman is the plural word for mother. I use both in the text of this chapter.

3. In Anishinaabe culture, maternal caregivers include mothers, grand mothers, aunties, Two-Spirited people, cousins, sisters, guardians, Elders, and so on.

4. Kwe is singular for women, females, or Two-Spirited people who identify as female; Kwewag is the plural version.

5. "Ban" is the Anishinaabe way of respectfully acknowledging an Anishinaabe individual who has passed away.

6. This word means Mother Earth. Spelling varies depending on the linguistic writing system used or the regional dialect.

7. I call myself a "river" Water Protector because my people are river people and live along the French River waterway that connects to Lake Nipissing. I grew up along the river, and it has fed my family for generations.

8. In this paragraph, I share a variety of terminology. Some of this terminology is found in Sioux Lookout Meno Ya Win Health Centre, *Ojibwe Medical Dictionary: A Handbook for Health Care Providers*. The document is a valuable source of language education on anatomy within Anishinaabe contexts.

9. The first time I saw the term "Windigo economies" was in Robin Kimmerer's *Braiding Sweetgrass: Indigenous Wisdom, Scientific Knowledge and the Teachings of Plants*.

10. The copper in the pail of water is believed to have spiritual and medicinal healing qualities in that it works to purify the water. During the ceremony, water is placed in the copper pail, carried into ceremonies, and is treated like a relative. It is prayed to, sung to, and given an honoured place in the gathering. Women are the carriers

of the copper pail and water to honour the shared life-giving aspects of both.

Works Cited

"Anishinaabe Water Walkers Trek from Minnesota to Quebec to Honor Great Lakes." *Mother Earth Water Walk*, 21 July 2017, www.motherearthwaterwalk.com/?p=2865. Accessed 23 May 2020.

Bellow, Heather. "Native American Activist and Water Protector Winona LaDuke to Speak in Great Barrington." *The Berkshire Eagle*, 11 May 2018, www.berkshireeagle.com/stories/native-american-activist-and-water-protector-winona-laduke-to-speak-in-great-barrington,523527. Accessed 23 May 2020.

Benton-Banai, Edward. *The Mishomis Book: the Voice of the Ojibway.* Indian Country Press, 1979.

Borrows, John. *Canada's Indigenous Constitution.* University Press of Toronto Press, 2010.

Cook, Katsi. "Women are the First Environment." *Indian Country Today*, 23 Dec. 2003, indiancountrytoday.com/archive/cook-women-are-the-first-environment-bZbKXN9CME-UabNOEh Kgqg. Accessed 3 Jun. 2020.

Couchie, Carol, and Herb Nabigon. "A Path towards Reclaiming Nishnawbe Birth Culture: Can the Midwifery Exemption Clause for Aboriginal Midwives Make a Difference?" *The New Midwife: Reflections on Renaissance and Regulation*, edited by Farah M. Shroff, Women's Press, 1997, pp. 41-49.

Davidson-Hunt, Iain J., et al. "Iskatewizaagegan (Shoal Lake) Plant Knowledge: An Anishinaabe (Ojibway) Ethnobotany of Northwestern Ontario." *Journal of Ethnobiology.* vol. 25, no. 2, Fall/Winter 2005, pp. 189-227.

Dumont, James, "Journey to Daylight-land: Through Ojibwa Eyes," *Laurentian Review*, vol. 8, no. 2, 1976, pp. 31-34.

Geniusz, Wendy Makoons. *Our Knowledge Is Not Primitive: Decolonizing Botanical Anishinaabe Teachings.* Syracuse University Press, 2009.

"Grandmother Josephine Mandamin: A 69 Year Old Who Walked around the Great Lakes Talks about the Water Docs International Festival." *SheDoesTheCity*, 22 Mar. 2013, www.shedoesthecity.com/

grandmother-josephine-mandamin-a-69-year-old-who-walked-around-the-great-lakes-talks-about-the-water-docs-international-festival. Accessed 23 May 2020.

Johnson, Rhiannon. "'It's Really Very Crucial Right Now': Great Lakes Water Walk Focuses on Protecting 'Lifeblood.'" *CBC News*, Sept. 23 2017, www.cbc.ca/news/indigenous/great-lake-water-walk-meant-to-spread-awareness-open-to-all-1.4303050. Accessed 23 May 2020.

Johnston, Basil. *Ojibway Heritage*. McClelland and Stewart, 1976.

Johnston, Basil. *The Manitous: The Spiritual World of the Ojibway*. Key Porter Books, 1995.

Kapyrka, Julie. "'Nibi gi-zaagigoo'—Kawartha Water Walkers Honour the Otonabee River." *Anishinabek News*, 19 May 2015, anishinabe knews.ca/2015/05/19/nibi-gi-zaagigoo-kawartha-water-walkers-honour-the-otonabee-river/. Accessed 23 May 2020.

Kimmerer, Robin Wall. *Braiding Sweetgrass: Indigenous Wisdom, Scientific Knowledge and the Teachings of Plants*. Milkweed Editions, 2013.

LaDuke, Winona. *All Our Relations: Native Struggles for Land and Life*. South End Press, Honor the Earth, 1999.

LaDuke, Winona. "Anishinaabe Prophecy: Communities Must Choose the Green Path for Food, Energy." *Tribal Journal: Journal of American Indian Higher Education*. 15 Nov. 2008, tribalcollegejournal.org/anishinaabe-prophecy-communities-choose-green-path-food-energy/. Accessed 23 May 2020.

"Liz Oswamick Shares Her Water Song with the Roberston Program." *The Roberston Program*. 6 May 2016. wordpress.oise.utoronto.ca/robertson/2016/05/06/liz-osamawick-shares-her-water-song-with-the-robertson-program/. Accessed 23 May 2020.

"Liz Osawamick: Need to Get Back to the Old Ways." *YouTube*, uploaded by *Sacred Water*, 3 Feb. 2015, www.youtube.com/watch?v=ljDqEUvLKdA. Accessed Apr. 20, 2018.

Maracle, Lee. "Water." *Downstream: Reimagining Water*, edited by Dorothy Christian and Rita Wong, Wilfred Laurier University Press, pp. 33-28.

McGregor, Deborah. "Traditional Ecological Knowledge and Sustainable Development: Towards Co-Existence." *The Way of Development:*

Indigenous Peoples, Life Projects and Globalization, edited by Mario Blaser, Harvey A. Feit, and Glenn McRae, Zed Books, 2004, pp. 72-91.

"Meet Josephine Mandamin (Anishinaabekwe), The 'Water Walker.'" *Indigenous Rishing: An Indigenous Environmental Network Project*, 25 Sept. 2014, indigenousrising.org/josephine-mandamin/. Accessed 23 May 2020.

McMahon, Kevin. "A Native Grandmother's Epic Walk for the Water." The Star. 4 Apr. 2009. www.thestar.com/news/insight/2009/04/04/a_native_grandmothers_epic_walk_for_the_water.html. Accessed 23 Apr. 2018.

Mitchell, H.H., et al. "The Chemical Composition of the Adult Human Body and Its Bearing on the Biochemistry of Growth." *Division of Animal Nutrition, and the Departments of Physiology and Animal Husbandry. Journal of Biological Chemistry*, vol. 158, 1945, pp. 625-637.

Nabigon, Herb. *Hollow Tree: Fighting Addiction with Traditional Native Healing.* McGill-Queen's University Press, 2006.

"Nokomis Josephine Mandamin." *YouTube*, uploaded by Empty glassforwater, 23 Jun. 2010, www.youtube.com/watch?v=D6IcJZ9Wzuc. Accessed 23 May 2020.

"Pregnancy Amniotic Fluid." *YouTube*, uploaded by Pregnancy Chat, 20 Dec. 2011, www.youtube.com/watch?v=-AFyV-Descc. Accessed 23 May 2020.

Rheault, Darcy. "Anishinaabe Mino-Bimaadiziwin (The Way of a Good Me)." 1999.

"Seventh Annual Judith Davidson Moyers Women of Spirit Lecture." *YouTube*, uploaded by Union Theological Seminary, www.youtube.com/watch?v=sMEum7rlBIM&feature=youtu.be. Accessed 23 May 2020.

Sioux Lookout Meno Ya Win Health Centre, *Ojibwe Medical Dictionary A Handbook for Health Care Providers.* Sioux Lookout, 2011.

Simpson, Leanne *Dancing On Our Turtle's Back: Stories of Nishnaabeg Re-Creation, Resurgence and a New Emergence.* Arbeiter Ring Publications, 2011.

Thorpe, Dagmore. *People of the Seventh Fire.* Akwekon Press, 1996.

"Trekking the Great Lakes on Foot to Raise Awareness about Water Pollutants: Anishinawbe Grandmother Makes Final Marathon Water Walk." *CBC News*, 15 Jun. 2017, www.cbc.ca/news/canada/windsor/trekking-the-great-lakes-on-foot-to-raise-awareness-about-water-pollutants-1.4161467. Accessed 23 May 2020.

Trent University, PhD dissertation.

Vasil, Adria. "Great Lakes Water Walk Has Me Walking on Water." *Now Toronto*, 27 Sept. 2017, nowtoronto.com/lifestyle/ecoholic/great-lakes-water-walk-walking-on-water/. Accessed 23 May 2020.

Walkem, Ardith, "The Land is Dry: Indigenous Peoples, Water, and Environmental Justice," *Eau Canada: The Future of Canada's Water*, edited by Karen Baker, University of British Columbia Press, 2007, pp. 303-20.

Williams, Shirley. "7th Water Awareness Walk in the Kawarthas." *Indigenous Lands & Resources Today*, 19 May 2018, www.ilrtoday.ca/7th-water-awareness-walk-in-the-kawarthas/. Accessed 23 May 2020.

"Winona LaDuke—Honor the Earth—March 10, 2018." *YouTube*, uploaded by Talkingsticktv. 13 Mar. 2018, www.youtube.com/watch?v=b58Ont0S4QA&t=926s. Accessed 28 April 2018.

"Winona LaDuke Address Fargo—We are Water Protectors." *YouTube*, uploaded by Honor the Earth, 5 Sept. 2017, www.youtube.com/watch?v=Syyfe-lt2IA. Accessed 23 May 2020.

"Winona LaDuke with Love Water, Not Oil 2017 Wisconsin." *YouTube*, uploaded by IndianCountryTV, Aug. 18 2018, www.youtube.com/watch?v=CKy2evRZYDM. Accessed 23 May 2020.

Chapter Two

Mother Earth in Environmental Activism: Indigeneity, Maternal Thinking, and Animism in the Keystone Pipeline Debate

Rebecca Jaremko Bromwich

Introduction

If we seek gender equality and environmental protection as feminists, environmentalists, and activists should we use the term "Mother Earth"? This chapter engages this question, since certain feminist critics have seen the gendering of the earth as essentialist and drawing on problematic constructions of maternality. The thematic question this chapter seeks to address is one of great relevance for environmental advocates seeking to work simultaneously towards reducing levels of gender inequality. Sarah Milner-Barry and Sherri Ortner have contended that the discursive figure of Mother Nature reinforces the idea that both women and nature should be subjugated. They argue that value systems failing to value the natural environment as well as women are enmeshed and mutually supportive. Consequently, these value systems continue to reinforce imagery of Mother Nature and Mother Earth that serves to maintain the subjugation of women while legitimizing the exploitation and depletion of natural resources. This chapter asks whether it is unethical or unwise for those who seek gender equality to use the discursive figure of Mother Earth in environ-mental advocacy.

In this chapter, I critically explore the arguments against using the terms "Mother Earth" and "Mother Nature," with specific reference to their use in advocacy around the Keystone XL pipeline. The overarching question this chapter discusses is whether in environmental advocacy, the term "Mother Earth," as well as its undergirding construct of the earth as maternal, is sexist and should be abandoned. I employ critical discourse analysis of the conversations around the Keystone pipeline case to reveal the implications of using the figure of Mother Earth in environmental advocacy.

This chapter first uses critical discourse analysis to explore how the subjectivization of the earth as a mother through deployment of the discursive figure Mother Earth has been deployed in debates surrounding the Keystone XL pipeline. The chapter then reviews literature that critiques discursive configurations of the earth as maternal as well as considers the use of the Mother Earth construct in recent environmental advocacy and law reform. After situating the case study in this context, the chapter analyzes the representation effected by this construction, and its uses by advocates, in the Keystone XL case to address the question of whether feminist environmentalists should use or spurn the term.

I argue that the deployment of the discursive constructs of Mother Earth in environmental activism references and strengthens symbolic and ideological content from Indigenous worldviews and exist outside Western, patriarchal, and capitalist assumptions about what a mother is. The strategic deployment of the Mother Earth figure may neither be entirely unproblematic nor without risks, but it carries great potential to subvert capitalist and patriarchal logics. As deployed in contemporary environmental advocacy, this figure is given meaning within Indigenous, animist logics and should neither be dismissed as necessarily essentialist or disavowed as inevitably contributing to the continued subjection of women.

The Study: Critical Discourse Analysis

This chapter analyzes documents—advocacy, quasi-legal, and media—produced in North America about the Keystone XL pipeline between 2010 and 2018. The study was a qualitative critical discourse analysis conducted to ascertain how representations of the maternal and the Mother Earth construct have been deployed by advocates in the case of the Keystone XL pipeline. The configuration of the environment as a maternal subject in this event is used as a case study from which I explore the implications of using the maternal earth as a discursive construct for gender relations.

Critical discourse analysis is a methodological framework for conducting research into how discourses function as instruments of power and control. It looks at social structures and processes involved in text production and makes relationships of causality that are otherwise opaque clear and visible; critical discourse analysis highlights the links between texts and broader social and cultural power relations and discursive processes (Fairclough).

The dataset for the analysis was obtained via Google searches as well as the news database Factiva. Such search terms as "Keystone XL" "environment" "protest" "earth" and "Mother Earth" were variously used. A Google news search using the search terms "Keystone XL" and "Mother Earth" yielded 2,750 unique documents. The top one hundred articles from this Google search became the dataset used for this research. This study quantitatively and qualitatively analyzes how a variety of texts from sites of discursive production in media and legal discourses represented, articulated, and caused Mother Earth to emerge as a figure. It then critically analyses what figures of Mother Earth emerge in the texts, what public narratives and politics those figures support, and to what extent each configuration of Mother Earth is consistent or inconsistent with the philosophical orientation of maternal thinking.

For this work, I built on the method I used, and specifically the subject matter I studied, in my book analyzing discursive figures of mothers, girls, and inmates in the case of Ashley Smith, a young woman who died in a Canadian prison and whose death was ruled a homicide perpetrated by the criminal justice and correctional systems (Bromwich). The current study, like this prior work, explores what Lauren Berlant calls the "caseness" of figures of Mother Earth. The analysis involved asking of what figures of Mother Earth are constructed in the Keystone XL case.

I work with the concept of "figuration" (Laurentis), which is the process by which a representation is given a particular form: "A figure is the simultaneously material and semiotic product of certain [discursive] processes" (Casteneda, 3-4). A figuration is "a specific configuration of knowledges, practices and power" (Casteneda, 3-4). Accordingly, I qualitatively study media and legal texts to determine what figurations emerge in these cultural domains.

The term "maternal thinking" (Ruddick) is used in this chapter to refer to a particular strain of feminist theory developed in large part by philosopher Sara Ruddick and more recently expanded upon and clarified by leading Canadian motherhood scholar Andrea O'Reilly. As discussed by O'Reilly, Sara Ruddick, Patricia Hill Collins, and Adrienne Rich have helped to develop feminist motherhood theory. Ruddick sees maternal thinking as a discipline analogous to the discourses of religion or science with particular dimensions as a practice. Although traditionally under-stood as women's work, maternal thinking is not essentially female. It is a philosophical orientation that cognitively and performatively involves a kind of caring labour that is engaged and physical and that involves "protection, nurturance and training ... care and respect" (Ruddick 62). Ruddick identifies the "maternal standpoint" as a way of looking at all children and other people as human.

For Roddick, mothering is work, not an identity. She focuses on the performativity of maternal thinking and not on essential biological traits, thereby disaggregating maternalism from any particular embodied subject. She focuses not on static personal attributes but on themes characteristic of maternal thinking (Ruddick). Similarly, O'Reilly draws together Judith Butler's notions about the performativity of gender with Ruddick's maternal thinking to further advance a nonessentialist understanding of maternal activism. She writes that far from being essentially feminine, "motherhood is similarly performed by maternalist activists" (16). Maternal thinking is performed rather than biologically inhabited.

The Keystone Pipeline

The Keystone pipeline is an oil pipeline system linking Canada to the United States, which is related to, but not the same as, the Dakota Access pipeline. The Keystone Pipeline system runs from the Western

Canadian sedimentary basin, starting in Alberta, to refineries in Illinois and Texas and also to oil tank farms and to an oil pipeline distribution center in Cushing, Oklahoma (Keystone). This pipeline was first commissioned in 2010. At time of writing, in 2020, it is now owned solely by the TransCanada Corporation.

The pipeline became a controversial focus of public attention when a planned fourth phase, Keystone XL, attracted growing environmental protest. This phase of the project became, for many, a symbol not only in the battle over climate change and fossil fuels but also in the struggles of Indigenous peoples for self-determination. In 2015, the Keystone XL Pipeline was rejected by then President Barack Obama (Canadian Press). Environmental activists lauded this as a victory, but it was short lived. In January 24, 2017, newly elected President Donald Trump took action intended to permit the pipeline's completion by signing a presidential memorandum to that effect (Canadian Press). This decision, in turn, led to a new wave of Indigenous opposition.

Findings

This study confirms that configurations of the natural environment as a maternal subject were consistently dominant in the texts produced by activists opposing the development of the pipeline during the period studied. In short, discursive configuration of the earth as a mother in this case was powerful, emotionally resonant, and effective at galvanizing activism. Activists deployed a unitary, intersectional, and self-described Indigenous construct of Mother Earth, which remained consistent over time in the texts studied.

Although there were certainly some texts that referred to "the earth" rather than "Mother Earth" in advocacy, the dominant figuration of the natural environment in texts produced by activists in relation to the pipeline was as a mother, a female, and a maternal figure, which is not only anthropomorphic but also communitarian in nature. This was not an *ad hoc* synergy, nor was it a coincidence. In September 2011, opponents of the Keystone Pipeline approval signed reading "Mother Earth Accord" at the Rosebud Sioux Tribe Emergency Summit (IEN). This accord affirmed the Indigenous view "that the Earth is our true mother, our grandmother who gives birth to us and maintains all life," demanded a "moratorium on tar sands development," and rejected "the Presidential

Permit for the Keystone XL Pipeline" by Obama. (IEN)

In prior and subsequent texts, the use of the Mother Earth construct by Indigenous activists in opposition to the Keystone XL pipeline remained linked to indigeneity, which served not only to gender the earth but also to reference anticapitalist alternatives to viewing the environment as property. The construct fostered a sense of belonging, mutual accountability, and shared interests among the Indigenous activists as well as their allies.

In November 2015, when Obama announced that the Keystone Pipeline proposal would be rejected, the decision was widely hailed by activists as "a victory for Mother Earth" (Indigenous Environmental Network). Although it was only a temporary decision, as Trump reversed the decision in January 2017, as noted above, the discursive resonances and power of the figuration of the earth as a maternal subject remains evidently powerful.

Indeed, opposition to the Keystone XL pipeline, as revealed in this study, centred on the Mother Earth figure and the reciprocal relationship of caregiving, of Indigenous peoples as caretakers of her, and of her role as caregiver of life. The Mother Earth figure used by Indigenous activists is not simply a construction of personhood or femininity but a way of speaking about belonging and leadership. It is matched on several occasions by advocates referring to Obama as "the great white father" (e.g., White Plume). Mother Earth is, thus, presented as a counterpart to, or refutation of the power of, the patriarchal authority of colonial power.

The texts studied consistently framed Indigenous peoples' opposition to the Keystone pipeline as caretaking for Mother Earth. For example, in an article in *The Guardian*, activist Dallas Goldtooth identifies the figure of Mother Earth with Indigenous conceptions of an animistic worldview in which humans are part of nature and not separate from it:

> As Indigenous peoples, as Oceti Sakowin, we were handed down the original teachings on how to live in balance with Mother Earth. We must see all aspects of life as related, to respect the feminine principle of creation and to maintain a sustainable relationship with the land. These tenets are antithetical to the extractive economy we are faced with today. The land, air, and water are commodified. Mother Earth is being drilled, fracked, clear-cut, and destroyed with such brutality. We are on the brink of climate catastrophe. In order to avoid drastic climate change,

we need a moratorium on fossil fuel development and we need to invest in a zero carbon economy: our original teachings demand no less than this.

Advocates do not uniformly articulate the figure of Mother Earth. The articulations are nuanced and overwhelmingly intersectional; they link the maternality of the earth to the connection Indigenous peoples have with the environment. Consider this example: "The Earth is our Mother—she ain't going no place. In fact, Earth is an Indian mom; powerful, resilient, beautiful and will survive the very worst that the universe can give. Sure, she had it rough early on, but she's got that elasticity in her skin" (Ross).

Although the specific characteristics of the Mother Earth differ during the period studied, the configuration of the natural environment as a mother by advocates remains consistent. For instance, in 2017, after President Trump's approval of the Keystone XL pipeline, protests were unified around the Mother Earth figure and the role of Indigenous peoples in protecting here. A 2017 Declaration updating the 2011 Mother Earth Accord, which was signed by the Blackfoot Confederacy and Great Sioux Nation, opponents of the pipeline, says the following: "It is our turn to *use the voices that the colonizers understand* to say our mother the earth has withstood all that she should ever withstand on our behalf" (my emphasis, CBC News).

In 2017, a group calling itself the Treaty Alliance against the Tar Sands, which is composed of 150 First Nations across Canada and the United States, actively used the Mother Earth figure as a central, galvanizing concept in its environmental advocacy. Their 2016 Treaty Alliance against Tar Sands Expansion begins with a preamble that references Mother Earth and the need to protect it.

Contextualizing the Study

Critical Perspectives from Feminist Theory

Different lines of thought in feminist theory take divergent views on the configuration of the earth as a mother. Some feminists uncritically accept a naturalized view of the earth as feminine and seek to recuperate the subordinated feminine. Conversely, those who take a more social constructivist view of the cultural content of femininity reject the claim that nature is inherently feminine and problematize the discursive configuration of the earth as a mother. In feminist theoretical writing, gender essentialists and social constructivists often articulate the Mother Earth figure in their advocacy and rhetoric for different reasons. Gender essentialists tend to assume a naturalized connection of woman to nature and assume certain attributes to women and to nature that are shared; they see a central goal of feminism to be the recuperation and celebration of the feminine. Conversely, social constructivist feminist thinkers, such as Sherry Ortner, problematize the naturalization of traits conceived as feminine. Ortner contends in her 1974 article "Is Female to Male as Nature Is to Culture" that the association of women with nature is problematic because of its association of women with something societies devalue: "Woman is being identified with—or, if you will, seems to be a symbol of—something that every culture devalues, something that every culture defines as being of a lower order of existence than itself. Now it seems that there is only one thing that would fit that description, and that is 'nature' in the most generalized sense" (74).

Although there is a diversity of thought that considers itself to be ecofeminist, some of it being antiessentialist, many of the ecofeminists of the ecofeminism movement popular from 1970s through to the 1990s celebrated an essentialized connection of the sacred feminine to the natural environment (Sturgeon). In general, ecofeminists link the oppression of women to the oppression of animals and the natural environment; they have historically built on theories that femininity is associated with connectedness and nature, whereas masculinity is more associated with atomism and rights (Gaard).

However, a social constructivist approach does not necessarily find problematic configurations that relate the earth to having a female gender or maternal subjectivity.

For instance, Greta Gaard contends that the configuration of the earth as a mother has potential positive and negative effects. She asserts that on the positive side, conceptualizing the earth as a family member inspires humans to honour and care for the natural environment.

However, recent social constructivist feminist writing often criticizes the essentialization of the feminine and problematizes its association with nature. Several contemporary feminist scholars have argued that in the context of a patriarchal society, using the term "Mother Earth" and similar figurations of the natural environment as female and maternal encourages humanity to exploit and denigrate the earth in the same ways women are exploited; it also assumes that the earth, as our mother, will always nurture us. Sarah Milner-Barry, for example, has critiqued representations of the earth as a maternal figure: "Unfortunately, the idea that women and nature are inherently linked is a tacit acceptance of their mutual exploitation." In fairness, as Gaard discusses, ecofeminist theory generally shares the view that the linkage of women to nature in patriarchal discourses supports the oppression of women and the exploitation of nature. However, most ecofeminist thought is character- ized by some level of naturalization of the association of nature with the feminine and some level of essentialization of what it is to be a woman.

Critics of the use of the Mother Earth figure in environmental advocacy are often concerned that environmentalism involving a close association of women with nature invokes and reinscribes a nostalgic conception of preindustrial life, which masks the ways in which women were oppressed within it. For example, Jennifer Bernstein asks, "What would an environmentalism that takes feminism seriously look like?" She further contends the following:

> The glorification of nature and farming and the romanticizing of the home, domestic life, and the woman at the center of it are ultimately nostalgias that cover up the brutality of rural life and drudgery of domestic labor in a perfume of freshly cut hay and caramelizing onions. While the new domestics advocating home brewing, fermenting kombucha, and churning butter are likely aware of their irony in an era of unprecedented technological progress, this nostalgia does little to further the goals of middle- and lower-class women in the developed world.

Susan Schrepfer and Douglas Cazaux Sackman, too, are critical of the use of the Mother Earth construct in environmental advocacy. They showcase the link between "ecological imperialism and sexual subordination" (119)—the basis for the notion that both women and the earth are passive and ideal for domination (119) They argue further that "metaphors used to describe nature as mother ... reflect and reinforce social divisions ... [and] relations of dominance between men, women, and nature" (117).

These theorists argue that the association of nature with women and with maternal subjects, which has been used to ideologically justify the denigration of women, devalues nature. Milner-Barry argues that the configuration of the earth as a mother and the devaluation of tasks associated with maternality, such as birth giving and childrearing, supports both the subjugation of women and the degradation of the natural environment:

> The term "Mother Nature," then, although it arose from spiritually rich traditions, has come to represent the twinned exploitation of all that patriarchal society considers to be inferior to men. As such, both are expected to be perpetually available to them, and to be accepting and accommodating of their desires. As long as the reason for gendered oppression is rooted in women's apparent closeness to nature, this kind of rhetoric provides another reason to view both women and the Earth as existing on an unequal plane with men. (p. 35)

Indigenous Contexts and Legal Construct of "Mother Earth"

The Mother Earth figure features prominently in contemporary writing about environmental advocacy as articulated by Indigenous advocates and organizations. Furthermore, the Mother Earth figure has a nascent presence as a liminal being in international and some domestic law. In the last decade, Ecuador and Bolivia have constitutionally enshrined protections for Mother Earth, which is discussed below. Although ecofeminist writing has expressed concerns about the colonization of Indigenous worldviews by environmentalists (Gaard) through their use of the Mother Earth in activism, it is also important to note that Indigenous activists and communities frequently deploy the term "Mother Earth" themselves. The Mother Earth figure is also taking on a legal existence in a growing number of jurisdictions.

As a preliminary note, it is the subject of academic debate whether the Mother Earth figure, as a gendered and maternal personification of the natural environment, is a longstanding feature of North American Indigenous traditions. Some scholars have argued that it is not (Gill; Bierhorst); rather, they have contended that prior to contact with European settlers, Indigenous peoples in North America did not conceptualize the earth as female or maternal. Sam Gill traces the historical development of the Mother Earth figure in American

Indigenous traditions to argue that a theological construct of Mother Earth is not originally or fully Indigenous to North America. However, others have argued that to consider Gill's study as a refutation of the authenticity of Mother Earth as an Indigenous construct or figure is to misapprehend the nature of oral histories. Oral histories are crafted to engage with the present and invoke traditions in dynamic ways; they are not simply artefacts of the past (Gernet 11).

For the purposes of this analysis, Gill's critique of historical authenticity is not relevant. This is not a history or genealogy of the representation of Mother Earth; instead, this research asks in what ways the discursive construct of Mother Earth exists in the advocacy articulated by Indigenous peoples in North America today. It also looks at contemporary advocacy by people who, while not identifying as Indigenous, also fight against the Keystone Pipeline and at more general environmental advocacy that is framed in terms of Mother Earth as a figure. The Mother Earth figure is identified in this advocacy as an Indigenous concept, and it is constructed within logics that are claimed as Indigenous.

The maternality of the earth in Indigenous worldviews is not precisely the same thing as legal personhood for the earth. It is a broader conception of connectedness: it is bigger and more intimate than personhood. In general, most Indigenous advocates distinguish maternal configuration of the earth from granting it legal personhood and prefer using a configuration of Mother Earth over a genderless personhood for nature (RONWE 6). The configuration of the earth as a mother has legal dimensions in Indigenous advocacy. It references not just femininity but an animist conceptualization of the land that counters colonial concepts of property and property law, a sentiment that also been articulated as the principle "that land for Native Americans is a 'sacred and inalienable mother,' while for the whites it is a 'commodity'" (Washburn 143). The use of the "Mother Earth" construct in this logic is not simply a personification of the earth. It is grounded in Indigenous conceptions of the world as animistic: earth is not a mother in a human sense. Indeed, the Mother Earth figure is not an extension of personhood. As such, Indigenous configurations of Mother Earth do not represent the colonization of the natural world with an analog to human rights discourse; these representations are not simply making the world into a human being. As John Burrows discusses, Indigenous traditions in

Canada work from a worldview in which the earth is not an inanimate piece of property but rather a living being. Further, Burrows sees the animate, and not proprietary, nature of the earth as a configuration that is legal and is part of Indigenous law. In Indigenous legal traditions, the earth has a status that is nonhuman and legal.

The legal reconstitution of the natural world from human property into a rights-bearing entity is being driven, in many contexts, by the personification of the earth not as a human generally but as a mother specifically. Recent shifts in environmental regulation in several jurisdictions have invoked and deployed the Mother Earth figure. The Universal Declaration on the Rights of Mother Earth was presented at the World People's Conference on Climate Change and the Rights of Mother Earth, at Cochabamba, Bolivia, on April 22, 2010. It commences with a configuration of Mother Earth as follows: "We are all part of Mother Earth, an indivisible, living community of interrelated and interdependent beings with a common destiny."

In this legal construction, Mother Earth is configured not as a human being, or not only as a human being, but as a community. The figure has the relational and gestational attributes characteristic of an expectant mother. This configuration uses the concept of motherhood to interrupt the logic of the construction of atomistic human rights. It is not an outgrowth of, or an analogy to, human rights.

The underlying logics behind constructions of Mother Earth are indeed different from the logics of capitalism. The Declaration goes on to say: "The capitalist system and all forms of depredation, exploitation, abuse and contamination have caused great destruction, degradation and disruption of Mother Earth, putting life as we know it today at risk through phenomena such as climate change." As noted above, Mother Earth is a figure around which nascent legal cultures are developing across jurisdictions, especially in Latin America. In Bolivia, the Framework Law of Mother Earth and Integral Development to Live Well was enacted in 2012, after the country adopted a new constitution in 2009, as part of a complete restructuring of the Bolivian legal system (Hindery). This law reform has been heavily influenced by a resurgent Indigenous Andean spiritual worldview, which places the environment and the earth deity known as the Pachamama at the centre of all life. In this worldview, as expressed in the Law of Mother Earth, humans are considered equal to, and linked with, all other entities and are not set apart from nature (Hindery). In Ecuador, the figure of Pachamama, an Inca maternal deity symbolic of earth's fecundity, was introduced into the country's constitution in 2008 as a figure around which the rights of nature "to exist, persist, maintain and regenerate its vital cycles" are constructed (Berros). In both the Bolivian and Ecuadorian instances, Mother Earth is characterized as a community of living things.

Analysis of the Keystone Case

The Mother Earth figure used by advocates opposing the Keystone XL pipeline clearly represents the animist configuration of the natural world found in Indigenous advocacy more generally. This is one case of a more general type, in which the Mother Earth figure grounded in animist worldviews that are self-identified as Indigenous is emergent as a legal persona or rights-bearing entity. As an entity, Mother Earth, as articulated in the Keystone XL case, has gendered content. However, its gender and maternality are given meaning through systems of logic that are identified as Indigenous. These systems of logic are not the same as those that have produced gender inequality in the Western, industrialized, and capitalist world. Thus, those with feminist agendas should embrace the use of the Mother Earth figure for its revolutionary potential to interrupt and subvert capitalist, consumerist, and colonial notions of value in intersectional ways.

This analysis suggests that rather than swearing off using the maternal subjectivization of the natural world, feminist environmental activists would be wiser to deploy it in animistic and anticapitalist theoretical and logical frameworks. Instead of articulating the Mother Earth figure on its own, it may be better to also describe the concepts this figure intends to convey directly. It might be preferable to talk expressly about maternal thinking, caregiving labour, the motherwork, of the earth, and our belonging to it, rather than assuming that content is inherently signified by the construct of Mother Earth. The deployment of the discursive figure of Mother Earth is also a means to appeal to what Ruddick has identified as "maternal thinking"—a different way to conceptualize the embodiment and interdependency of humans and the natural world. The animistic conception of the earth as a mother that is found in the Indigenous advocacy opposing the Keystone XL pipeline resembles maternal thinking in that they both invoke ideas of belonging and accountability through interconnectedness.

Ubiquitous and powerful in environmental advocacy, The Mother Earth figure is not simply a person. It exceeds personhood. It is not simply an anthropomorphization that acquires rights and attributes of those of a female human being. Rather, it is a relational description of the connection that people have to earth. The metaphor of motherhood, with its gestational and communitarian implications, speaks back against capitalism and atomism in effective ways. The configuration in advocacy and legal discourse of Mother Earth is powerful in challenging precisely what troubles Sheryl Hamilton in her book *Impersonations*: the modernist binaries between nature and culture, object and subject. Thus, the configuration of the earth as a mother is a powerful discursive technology.

The configuration of earth as Mother Earth can play upon the benefits of legal personhood while subverting the capitalist philosophy beneath it. It is useful to think of the Mother Earth figure not as a person but as a member of a broader category of what Hamilton class "persona"—a "liminal being," an entity capable of bearing rights that is not restricted to a "particular physical form" (21). As Hamilton argues, it is around these liminal beings that important social questions are worked through.

Equally, as Hamilton notes, the production of social personae can have unintended results. Hamilton cautions that the use of the Mother Earth figure in environmental advocacy may undermine the significance of the environment when it intersects with capitalism (30). However, it may also have an opposite effect. If Mother Earth is important, may this potentially trouble the undermining and undervaluing of unpaid labour performed by mothers within capitalism? The use of the Mother Earth construct provides a legible, or at least semilegible, discursive figure that can resonate with colonial ideas to some degree. It is proving to be a tenacious and powerful discursive technology in the battles against corporate and colonial power. Moreover, non-Indigenous advocates for better environmental stewardship have no right to discipline or police the language used by Indigenous ones.

Postcolonial feminist philosopher and literary theorist Gayatri Chakravorty Spivak first coined the term strategic essentialism, which is undertaken intentionally by activists and advocates when they provisionally accept essentialist foundations for certain categories of identity as a strategy for collective representation in order to pursue their political ends. Even if feminists are concerned about the possible consequences of using Mother Earth and other maternal figurations of the natural environment, the power of the figure, as evidenced in recent Latin American law reform, means that it should not be dismissed or ignored by advocates as a tool, but the question of colonial appropriation of Indigenous ideas (Gaard) does merit critical exploration if advocates consider using the figuration. However, this study of the deployment of the Mother Earth figure in the Keystone XL pipeline debate shows the governmental efficacy of discursive configuration of the earth as maternal. The strategic deployment of the maternal figures of earth has been effectively used in the Keystone XL Pipeline case in negotiating power and control over the natural world, and it can be predictably and effectively used on a continuing basis.

Conclusion

In short, the research presented in this chapter answers the question of whether environmental advocates who also seek gender equality should use the term "Mother Earth" with a resounding "yes." This analysis does not dispute the social constructivist theoretical point that assigning a gender and role to the earth is not inevitable and is to some extent arbitrary. This critical discourse analysis of the debates surrounding the Keystone XL pipeline shows that the configuration of the earth as a maternal subject, while it may be problematic, is also more complicated than simply being about gender. Perhaps, most importantly, the Mother Earth figure as a representation in discourse is a powerful resource.

This chapter has performed a critical discourse analysis of the uses, impact, and symbolic content of the discursive Mother Earth figure as deployed in the case of the Keystone Pipeline. It has critically assessed to what extent Western assumptions about mothers and gender are reinscribed by the deployment of this figure in advocacy and has revealed that the use of the Mother Earth figure in this case invokes and draws on notions of belonging and indigeneity that extend beyond legal personhood and female gender. As deployed by advocates in the Keystone XL pipeline case, the Mother Earth figure does not draw on but rather interrupts and unsettles colonial, settler assumptions about gender and maternality. Thus, rather than reinscribing patriarchal, capitalist logics, the Mother Earth figure has revolutionary potential to fundamentally trouble them.

This study has shown that contemporary discursive constructs of the earth as maternal in environmental activism draw largely on animistic conceptions of the earth found in Indigenous traditions rather than purely on Western notions of male and female, which Ortner and Milner-Berry are concerned about. Thus, these configurations do not necessarily carry the same stigmatizing or subordinating cultural baggage. Indeed, Ortner and Milner-Berry's arguments against use of the term "Mother Earth" in environmental advocacy and counter to deployments of maternal figures of the natural environment seem to be ethnocentric and colonial in their understandings of what mothers are and can be.

The symbolic content of the Mother Earth figure in the advocacy around the Keystone XL case is not delimited by Western notions of maternality in its expression. However, this discursive figure does carry the potential to be received by Western listeners in the problematic ways that Milner-Barry and Ortner contend. To avoid the devaluation of the earth or femininity that these feminist theorists warn against, it may be wise for advocates speaking from outside of Indigenous traditions to explicitly ground deployments of the Mother Earth figure in internationally referenced idea systems. In my view, on the basis of this study, Western feminist environmentalists should, when employing the term "Mother Earth," reference not only maternality but also the implicit notions of belonging, connectedness, and animism that are invoked in by the term when used by Indigenous activists. It is, ultimately, not the construction of the earth as feminine but the notion of maternality in referencing our rootedness and belonging to her that most clearly undermines the capitalist and patriarchal logics supporting exploitation.

Work Cited

Berlant, Lauren. "On the Case." *Critical Inquiry* vol. 33 no. 4, 2007, pp. 663-72.

Bernstein, Sarah, "Why Environmentalism Has a Gender Problem." *Communists in Situ.* cominsitu.wordpress.com/2017/09/06/on-mother-earth-and-earth-mothers/. Accessed 25 May 2020.

Berros, María Valeria. "The Constitution of the Republic of Ecuador: Pachamama Has Rights." *Environment & Society Portal*, no. 11, Arcadia, Rachel Carson Center for Environment and Society, 2015.

Bierhorst, John. *Way of the Earth: Native America and the Environment.* William Morrow, 1994.

Bromwich, Rebecca. *Looking for Ashley: Re-Reading What the Smith Case Reveals about the Governance of Girls, Mothers and Families in Canada.* Demeter Press, 2015.

Burrows, J. (2008). "Living Law on a Living Earth: Aboriginal Religion, Law, and the Constitution." *Law and Religious Pluralism in Canada*, edited by R. Moon, UBC Press, 2008, pp. 161-191.

Canadian Press, "A Chronological History of Controversial Keystone XL Pipeline Project." *CBC News*, 2017, www.cbc.ca/news/politics/keystone-xl-pipeline-timeline-1.3950156. Accessed 25 May 2020.

Castaneda, Claudia. *Figurations: Child, Bodies, Worlds.* Duke University Press, 2002.

CBC News "Indigenous Leaders Sign Opposition to Keystone XL in Calgary" *CBC News,* 17 May 2017, www.cbc.ca/news/canada/calgary/transcanada-keystone-calgary-indigenous-1.4119301. Accessed 25 May 2020.

Lauretis, Teresa de. *Figures of Resistance: Essays in Feminist Theory.* University of Illinois Press, 2007.

Fairclough, Norman. *Critical Discourse Analysis: The Critical Study of Language.* Longman, 1995.

Gaard, Greta, ed. *Women, Animals, Nature.* Temple University Press, 1993.

Gernet, Alexander von. *Oral Narratives and Aboriginal Pasts: An Interdisciplinary Review of the Literature on Oral Traditions and Oral Histories.* Department of Indian and Northern Affairs, April 1996.

Gill, Sam, *Mother Earth: An American Story.* University of Chicago Press, 1987.

Goldtooth, Dallas, "Keystone XL Would Destroy Our Native Lands. This Is Why We Fight." *The Guardian*, 9 Jan. 2015, www.theguardian.com/commentisfree/2015/jan/09/keystone-xl-would-destroy-native-lands-we-fight. Accessed 25 May 2020.

Hamilton, Sheryl, *Impersonations: Troubling the Person in Law and Culture.* University of Toronto Press.

Hindery, Derrick, *From Enron to Evo: Pipeline Politics, Global Environmentalism, andIndigenous Rights in Bolivia.* University of Arizona Press, 2013.

IEN, "Mother Earth Accord." Rosebud Sioux Tribe Emergency Summit, *IEN,* 2011, www.ienearth.org/mother-earth-accord/. Accessed 25 May 2020.

Johnson, Rebecca. *Taxing Choices: The Intersection of Class, Gender, Parenthood and the Law.* University of British Columbia Press, 2002.

"Keystone Pipeline System." *TransCanada.* www.tcenergy.com/operations/oil-and-liquids/keystone-pipeline-system/. Accessed 1 June 2020.

Milner-Barry, Sarah. "The Term 'Mother Nature' Reinforces the Idea That Both Women and Nature Should Be Subjugated." *Space Stereotypes,* qz.com/562833/the-term-mother-nature-reinforces-the-idea-that-both-women-and-nature-should-be-subjugated/. Accessed 25 May 2020.

Ortner, Sherry B. "Is Female to Male as Nature Is to Culture? *Woman, Culture, and Society,* edited by M. Z. Rosaldo and L. Lamphere, Stanford University Press, 1974, pp. 68-87.

O'Reilly, Andrea. *The Twenty-First Century Motherhood Movement.* Demeter Press, 2011.

Ross, Gyassi, "Keystone XL and Protecting Mother Earth: A Fight All Native People Should Fight." Tulalip News, Apr. 22 2014, www.tulalipnews.com/wp/2014/04/22/keystone-xl-and-protecting-mother-earth-a-fight-all-native-people-should-fight/. Accessed 1 June 2020.

Ruddick, Sara. *Maternal Thinking: Toward a Politics of Peace.* Beacon Press, 1995.

Schrepfer, Susan R. and Douglas Cazaux Sackman. *A Companion to American Environmental History.* Wiley-Blackwell, 2010.

Spivak, Gayatri. *The Post-colonial Critic: Interviews, Strategies, Dialogues.* Routledge, 1990.

Sturgeon, Noel. *Ecofeminist Natures: Race, Gender, Feminist Theory and Political Action.* Routledge, 1997.

"Treaty Alliance against Tar Sands Expansion." *Treaty Alliance,* 2016, www.treatyalliance.org/wp-content/uploads/2016/12/Treatyand AdditionalInformation-20161216-OL.pdf. Accessed 25 May 2020.

White Plume, Debra. "Testimony at the Public Hearing on the 1600 Mile TransCanada Pipeline." U.S. State Department, *YouTube,* Oct.

7 2011, www.youtube.com/watch?time_continue=228&v= wJc5X
PQXSCY.

Washburn, Wilcomb E. *Red Man's Land—White Man's Law*. Scribner,
1971.

Part II

Tensions in Maternal Activism

The Many Hands of Motherhood

Dara Herman Zierlein

Chapter Three

Almira and Me: Remembering the Maternalist Roots of Almira Hart Lincoln Phelps

Karen I. Case

Almost two hundred years after the publication of Almira Hart Lincoln Phelps's *Familiar Lectures on Botany*, I stood in a spring garden with Avery, who righteously informed me that the Crocus I had just pointed out to her was in actuality a Snowdrop. According to Almira's text, the Snowdrop has "Petals 3...stigma simple" (Lincoln 351). The Crocus "has a bulbous root, long and narrow leaves ... six petals" appearing as early as March" (Lincoln 201). Avery's birthday is in March, and that afternoon she had just finished her cake and fifth year. I counted three petals. Avery was correct. It was a Snowdrop. I asked her to thank Almira Hart Lincoln Phelps and before turning to scare the squirrel from the feeder, Avery asked, "Who's that?"

A Connecticut-born, nineteenth-century botanist, textbook author, novelist, and proponent of women's education, Almira once stated that "If we had no sciences, nature would present exactly the same phenomena as present.... Some relations or resemblances seen at first glance; others not discovered until after close examination and reflection" (Lincoln 13). The same may be said for my investigation into her work and its relationship to mothering, ecofeminism, and ecofeminist pedagogy. Born to older parents in Berlin, Connecticut, on July 15, 1793, Almira was the seventeenth and last child of Samuel Hart and Lydia Hinsdale Hart.

Samuel Hart, a man described as "dangerously liberal" (Bartlett 556) was fifty-five when Almira was born. Her mother, Lydia Hart, "a woman of great energy and sound judgment" (Hale and Adams 610) was forty-six—"one of the notable New England housekeepers" at the "ready to give searching criticism to the Sunday sermon, or kind and effective service to a sick neighbor" (Bartlett 556). Almira was six years the junior of her sister, Emma Hart Willard, a more well-known proponent of women's education and founder of Troy Female Seminary, later the Emma Willard School. It was one of the first schools in the United State to provide women with a comparable education to men. One writer noted "Where Mrs. Almira Lincoln Phelps has been known at all it has been as the sister, and perhaps shadow, of Emma Willard" (Good 222).

The word "shadow" acts as noun and verb. A darkened shape created by an object coming between light and a surface, "shadow" can also mean the close observation of someone. Biographical writing is like the shadowing of someone. Its intimate nature is rooted partially in the subjective (Bell and Yalom 3), with the boundaries between the biographical and autobiographical becoming murky. Although Almira and I had to have shared an affinity of sorts due to my initial interest, our resemblance was not necessarily apparent at the onset. My previous scholarship examines the naturalist intelligence of children with attention deficit hyperactivity disorder (ADHD) and the maternal pedagogies that support them. Nature or green spaces soothe children with ADHD. Gardens make superb pedagogical tools, as they offer students an opportunity to hyper focus on plants in a calming space. I thought that this was perhaps my connection to Almira.

Throughout my reading of her texts and biography, I vacillated. I liked her. I didn't like her. I felt a need to reimagine her mothering and relationship to plants and the broader natural world. Ann Firor Scott writes in *Making the Invisible Woman Visible* that "People who were not frightened by Almira Lincoln's forceful personality often found her magnetic" (95). Almira seemed to be an admonishing "all mother," and I found her compelling but wondered about what Scott termed her "darker side," which she kept controlled and out of public scrutiny (103). Like most republican mothers of the time period, Almira exhibited herself as ever dutiful. During my working, driving, and leisure hours, she presented a ghostly stoicism, expecting me to live without complaint or hysteria over President Trump's degradation of women and the environment. Almira's text, *Familiar Lectures on Botany*, was like my garden for ADHD students, as tranquil as it was enchanting.

It is said that Almira's overall writings were a "way to inscribe women's power through domestic influence" (Eldred and Mortensen 145). However, I found this designation too facile, given her contradictory positions as proponent of women's education and antisuffragette. Actively engaged in theorizing women's relationship to the natural world, Almira believed that women had a dual responsibility to be scientific observers and recognizers of the "the moral and sentimental intricacies of nature" (Gianquitto 21). Today, she is still an ambiguous and contradictory figure. During her time, she provided a consistent public narrative that informed young women about living in the domestic, public, spiritual and natural realm. I'd joke with colleagues that when writing I worried she'd haunt my keyboard. When not writing, I feared her spectral animosity if I engaged in the trivial. Almira intimidated, insinuating herself onto every page. She wrote, "It is unfortunately too much the case, that female ingenuity ... is in a great degree directed to trivial objects ... But a taste for scientific pursuits once acquired, a lady will feel that she has not time for engagements, which neither tend to the good of others, nor make herself wiser or better" (Lincoln 32).

Ironically, tending "to the good of others" may have contributed to the "invisibility problem" of many women scientists in the nineteenth century. Although their activities were scientific in nature, they often occurred in the domestic sphere outside the realm of science. Nineteenth-century female scientists had a "camouflage intentionally placed over their presence" (Rossiter xv) and this was particularly true for female botanists and might also be said of the plant world. Plants, like women, have been "profoundly backgrounded in most of Western thought and life" requiring "particular methodological sensitivities to their invisibility" (Head et al. 864).

Almira blurred distinctions between the vegetal and animal world, foreshadowing what has been defined as "plant blindness": "We should not infer, because the design for which they have been formed is in some measure concealed from us, that they were made for no purpose, or exist by mere accident; let us rather with humility acknowledge that this blindness must be owing to the limited nature of our own faculties" (Lincoln 63). John Charles Ryan writes in *Plants in Contemporary Poetry: Ecocriticism and the Botanical Imagination* that by "(re) turning human attention to botanical beings, critical plant studies ... attempts to reverse the tendency denoted as plant blindness." He continues: "As man's inclination to overlook flora, to undervalue its global biocultural significance, or to render it appropriable matter in service to human desire, plant blindness highlights the physiological limits of visual processing in humans" (6).

Following Darwin's lead, Almira wrote of plants exhibiting sensations: "The sensitive plant shrinks from touch; the Dionea suddenly closes its leaves upon the insect which touches them ... does there not seem as much appearance of sensation and instinct, and even more than in the lower orders of animals" (Lincoln 244). Evolutionary ecologist, Monica Gagliano, along with a research team, examined the sensitive plant, the Momosa Pudica, mentioned by Almira. In an experiment, they found the sensitive plant's leaf-folding behaviour in response to repeated disturbance indicated a possible persistent habituation or form of nonassociative learning. Gagliano states, "We tend not to credit plants with intelligence simply out of habit, because most of us remain plant blind: If you want to see plants as something that can never do anything purposefully, that's what you are going to see" (qtd. in Zaraska 57). Almira, in a passage titled "The Child in Nature" contends that "Our emotions have become blinded by habit. We do not admire what is familiar to us, and therefore it is, that we must be ever ignorant of the true native sympathy between our own hearts and the external world" (qtd. in Hart 110).

Current scientific understandings have their foundations in the past, and the study of women scientists' lives can provide insights into forces working against their professional success. Almira was not considered a true botanist. Frank Crosswhite and Carol Crosswhite state that Californian Katherine Brandegee was the only real American woman plant scientist of the nineteenth century. They maintain that other women during this time were "shunted into writing books for women or children" (128), which was considered a proper female undertaking (Larsen 2). Almira would have taken umbrage at the limited audience.

Emily Dickinson and Ralph Waldo Emerson read and held copies of Almira's *Familiar Lectures on Botany* in their libraries. Dickinson biographer, Sewall, writes "it may well have been one of the most important of her school books. Here were no lessons to be learned by rote, but (for Emily) a life-giving source" (351). Emerson also used the book as a reference for his essay "Compensation," in which he compared the roots of the Banyan tree to the human gains derived from loss. Emerson writes that individuals who have not experienced loss are like a "sunny garden-flower, with no room for its roots and too much sunshine for its head" (qtd. in Kuiken 22). It is "by falling off the walls and the neglect of the gardener is made the banian of the forest, yielding shade and fruit to wide neighborhoods of men" (Emerson qtd. in Kuiken 22). Emerson could not have seen this tree in America at the time, so he must have encountered the description and illustration in his annotated copy of *Familiar Lectures on Botany*. Almira states the tree is "a remarkable phenomenon." The stems "throw out fibres, which descend and take root in the earth. In a process of time, they become large trees; and thus, from one primitive root is formed a little forest" (Lincoln 63). Today, a seven-hundred-year-old Bayan in India, named "Pillalamarri," or the children's tree, encompasses three acres and subsists on an insecticide drip. Indian officials have been blocking the area from tourists (Apparasu). The current state of the Bayan tree has proven Emerson wrong. The neglect of the gardener can kill the tree.

Historians of science have paid little consideration to how the personal lives of women are rooted in their careers (Abir-Am and Outram 1), despite the boundaries between their public and private spheres being rather permeable (Blackmore 29). This is true of Almira. Like the Banyan tree, she stretched the boundaries of the domestic sphere "beyond recognition" while attesting to the need for margins (Scott 92). She "used the natural world as a platform for discussing issues of domesticity, education, morality, and the nation" (Gianquitto i). Considered female environmental "evangelicals," women scientists and naturalists were seen as "helpers to male scientists, and collectors, or popularizers rather than as producers of scientific knowledge" (Tolley 101). The designation of "popularization" fails to adequately represent the "rich variety of activities, sites and experiences in the heterogeneous culture of the nineteenth-century science; both to the importance of these practices and publications to defining and articulating what science was" (Keene 54). Nineteenth-century texts were often labelled "familiar," encompassing a myriad of disciplines. These books were marked by a "conversational language, a particular kind of domestic experience, and a particular kind of embodied relationship between the book and its reader" (Keene, 56). Science textbooks, like *Familiar Lectures on*

Botany, which held the label "familiar" employed the vernacular and used everyday objects and situations to achieve explanatory ends" (Keene 54) within the home.

The family home of domicile became the locus for botanical activity in the nineteenth century. The activity of botany consisted of elements conductive to family activity taking place inside and outside the domicile. Almira writes in Botany for Beginners that "Every person who would become a Botanist should preserve specimens of all the plants he meets with. A book of such specimens is called an herbarium. There are few parents that would not delight to see a handsome herbarium made by their child" (Phelps 21). Activities also occurred outside the home and Almira writes that "Young Botanists, as well as those who are older, may derive great pleasure in making excursions into the fields, and upon the hills and mountains for the purpose collecting plants" (Phelps 22). A description of Almira as a young teacher overseeing such an excursion appears in the History of Berlin, Connecticut.

> Over on the "Ledge," back of the old Bosworth place, sitting on a most bank, where the wind flowers grew, and partridge berries, and fragrant Pipsissewa. There, teacher gathered about her knee her class of little girls, who had begun to study the new botany and taught them to name the parts of the flowers, which they held in their hands. One of that lass placed a mark in the index of her book, against all the flowers she learned to know. There are 126 marks there (North 78-79).

Mothers as well as teachers played a central role in botanical activities and culture during the nineteenth century. Ann Shteir contends that botany was actually equated to good mothering (32), becoming so entwined that an illustration in the children's magazine *St. Nicholas*, edited by Mary Mapes Dodge, depicts a mother holding flowers over a baby in a carriage with the caption "First Class in Botany ... Please Rides" (Tolley 104). Mothering and service to the family still compromised women's highest priority. Phelps was advised by her mentor, Amos Eaton, cofounder of Rensselaer Polytechnic Institute, to write her first botany textbook in 1892. He later advised her that a woman's education was "as worthless as a fungus, if she is not more interested in the concerns of hers than in the concerns of the world" (Bollick 1). I suspect his guidance may have been due to jealousy over Almira's publication rates. Between 1835 and 1865, Phelps sold 375,000 copies of her botany textbooks as compared to the 18,000 texts sold by Eaton (Sundberg 103). Her texts far outsold the contemporary male authors of the time (Keeney 54). Despite her publication figures, Almira remained known as the protégé of Eaton, as opposed to a botanist in her own right. In a paper presented at the Torrey Botanical Club in 1909, John Hendley Barnhart recognizes Amos Eaton, stating his "manual, prepared specifically to meet the needs of the amateur, was popular for many years, and went through eight editions" (253). Barnhart acknowledges Almira as being among "the many inspired by him" (253).

Almira does not fare well in the contemporary opinions held by Robert Hendrick, a historian, and Emanuel Rudolph, a male botanist. Although Hendrick acknowledges that her writings reached tens of thousands, he considers her an opportunist, claiming she was "canny in the choice of her science" (296). Eaton, he maintains, was a leading scientist of the times (295). Contemporary botanist Rudolph describes Almira as "ordinary woman": "She was progressive, but not a revolutionary; she was an educational innovator, but not an educational reformer; and she was a scientific populizer but not a scientific investigator" (1161). Hendrick attacks those, similar to myself, who are attempting to revalue Almira's work: "It is today's historians, particularly those writing surveys of women's contribution to science, who tend to place her in the ranks of scientist" (298).

Almira was elected to the American Association for the Advancement of Science in 1859, and in 1874, she attended a reading of one of her papers by Professor Morse at the American Association for the Advancement of Science in Hartford Connecticut. During these meetings, women were not permitted to present their own work, and, thus, a male member would read their papers aloud to the audience. He depicted Almira as a "white-haired, pleasant-faced, very elderly lady" and added that it was "a rare sight indeed to see a lady past eighty with mind clear, and brain active on all questions of science (qtd. in Beach 492).

His dismissal of Almira's talents and may be due to the late nineteenth-century botany world having been divided between botanists, namely male scientists, and botanizers, consisting of female enthusiasts (Shteir 32). To dispel what was considered women's lack of objectivity, a "new botany" was proposed, which stressed scientific thinking through "laboratory instruction and rigor." This new botany was contrasted with "nature study," which was undertaken by female naturalists who underscored the appreciation of the natural world through direct observation (Keeney 68). Labelled "botanizers," female botanists were believed to be contributing to the feminization of botany (Keeney 70). Lois Arnold describes this as a move "from 'observational' botanical natural history based on morphology to a 'physiological' botany based on experimentation ... with the overall effect of taking botany from the multitude and confining it to the learned (15). This view negates the diffusion of scientific work by an American public (Thurs 41), who today could be considered citizen scientists.

There were both male and female botany enthusiasts in the nineteenth century; some collected plants for enjoyment, others for enlightenment, and still others as a means of admiring the handiwork of God (Keeney 1). Almira blended all three in her botanical writings and maintained that "of all the sciences, perhaps no one is settled on a firmer foundation than that of Botany" (Phelps 220). Botany, according to Almira, was "peculiarly adapted to females; the objects of its investigation are beautiful and delicate" (Lincoln 4).

Women and botanical subjects have long been tied together (McLeod), just not in the way Almira would have ever recognized. Patricia Fara calls botany, "sexy, dangerous—and big business" (44). Entwined with the fecund, the classic analogy of plants and women is the comparison of the "gravid female to the swelling fruit that contains a seed" (Taiz and Taiz viii). Prudence Gibson and Monica Gagliana argue that "Women have been associated with the blooming of flowers, the blossoming of buds, the genitalia of flowers as being female with the male stamen rising up out of it" (137). For Foucault, the field of botany and Linnaean taxonomy heralded the turnover of the premodern world into that of the modern. Whereas plants provided insight into the mysterious and "hidden relations among all nature" (Kelley 4), the advent of the Linnaean system exposed these associations via diagramming. Linnaeus's publication of the *Species Plantarum* in 1753 laid the groundwork for a botanic taxonomy based on male and female reproductive organs. Erasmus Darwin (grandfather of Charles) wrote *The Loves of Plants*, a poem in two volumes which provided a "vindication and explanation, both amusing and instructive, of Linnaeus's classification scheme for plants," portraying stamens and pistils as male and female sex organs (Browne 594). Fredrika Teute argues that "Attempts to propound a new order of personal relations founded on innate, universal characteristics paralleled the scientific quest to classify the natural world" (320). Implanted throughout these writings "was a clarion call for social progress, linking scientific knowledge with institutional critique and sexual freedom" (Teute 320) as well as a desire to conquer, subdue and deflower in the name of the British Empire (Fara).

These works were also construed by some male readers as pornographic (Fara), attracting the ire of eighteenth-century cleric and poet Richard Polwhele, who, among others, forecast the ruin of female purity due to women's enthusiasm for collecting and studying plants. Greta LaFleur suggests that Polwhele's series of images in poems—describing "heaving bosoms, "forbidden fruit," "pant[ing]," "prostitution," and the plant's "organ of unhallow'd lust"—might have rendered his work as perhaps more pornographic than the original (LeFluer 94). His description of female plant collectors as being rife "with bliss botanic as their bosoms heave [they] Still pluck forbidden fruit, with mother Eve" (LeFluer 94) edges toward his own sexual fantasy regarding Eve and the female plant collectors surrounding her.

Embodying the "prototypical" woman and mother (Frank 114), "Mother Eve" is rooted in botany as the first gardener. Traditionally, gardens have been associated with women and domestic activity, given the proximity of a garden to the home. Marijke van der Veen remarks that within a garden, there is an "intimacy of the daily tending of the plants that evokes similarities with that of rearing or nurturing children" (805). Given the absoluteness of Almira's Christian ethic, she was surprisingly understanding of Eve's expulsion from the garden. According to Almira, Eve "was assigned the pleasant task of giving names to flowers and numbering the tribes of plants" (Phelps 303) and upon banishment from the garden, she mourned their upkeep and abandonment Almira might have personalized Eve's loss of the garden. In a poem concerning Almira's leaving Vermont with her second husband, the Honorable John Phelps, to preside over a school located in Pennsylvania, Almira writes, "Flowers that I loved to tend, watching with care maternal for your bloom; Others may cull your sweets, enjoy your charms" (Phelps xxiv).

Maternal care and loss figure greatly in much of Almira's later writings and in her biographies, the most definitive one being a University of Pennsylvania dissertation by Emma Lydia Bolzau written in 1936.

Almira taught in a number of Connecticut schools between 1813 and 1817 until the age of twenty-four, when she married Simeon Lincoln, a Hartford printer on October 5, 1817. By the age of thirty, Almira had experienced the death of a year-old infant son, the birth of two daughters Jane and Emma, and the death of Simeon, who had contracted yellow fever and died at the age of thirty-three. Almira wrote the following lines from *The Complaint: of Night Thoughts of Life, Death and Immortality* by Edward Young on his gravestone: "Why then their loss deplore that are not lost? What though short his date?" (qtd. in J. Barber 67). A year later after settling her father-in-law and husband's estate, she joined her sister, Emma, at the Troy Female Seminary in New York as vice principal with daughters Jane (six) and Emma (two) in tow. Seven years later, she had completed *Familiar Lectures on Botany* and dedicated it to her mother—a woman Almira described as possessing an intellectual foundation that could be utilized to cross "the varied scenes of life" (iii). About her mother, she also writes, "Affection for my venerable parent induces me to dedicate to her, what will to her, be interesting, however it may be regarded by the severe of criticism" (iii).

In 1813, Almira married John Phelps, lawyer and widower with six children. They moved to Vermont where Almira gave birth to two children. During this time, she completed such works as *Geology for Beginners* (1832), *Female Student; or Fireside Friend* (1833), *Chemistry for Beginners* (1834), *Lectures on Natural Philosophy* (1835), *Lectures on Chemistry* (1837), and *Natural Philosophy for Beginners* (1837). It has been insinuated that Almira's productivity was directly related to her husband's lack of funds (Hendricks). Almira provided an alternate explanation: "Severe mental labor and close application, with consequent sedentary habits, having seriously affected her health, a change of climate and mode of life seemed desirable" (Phelps xix). They moved to oversee a seminary in West Chester, Pennsylvania. in 1838, a placement "regarded favorably by her husband" (Phelps xix). Given that the climate of Pennsylvania was equitable to Vermont's, Hendrick's supposition may likely be correct.

Almira presided over two additional female educational institutions, The Female Institute in Rahway, New Jersey in 1839 and for a more extended period, the Patapsco Female Institute from 1841 to 1856. It was at Patapsco in1849 that her husband John died. Almira writes that he "serenely passed away from earth, like the calm sun-set of an October evening" (Phelps xxi). Loss was a component of a single woman's live, but for Almira, unhappiness was magnified by marrying:

> Such is a woman's life! If she form no domestic ties, she sees, one by one, her early friends become engrossed with their families while her parents and other near relatives, one after another drop into the grave; she at length feels herself solitary and alone, in a world where are none to care for her; if she enter into the marriage state, she multiplies her chances of unhappiness, increases her cares, and becomes compelled to forget herself in her sacrifices for others; and often too without a return of gratitude and love from those for whom she has made the sacrifice ... the very term mother is one which involves the idea of suffering, anxiety, and love. (Phelps 137-38)

It was the death of her daughter, Jane Lincoln, in a train accident in Burlington, New Jersey, on August 29, 1885, that caused Almira to finally yield "to the pressure of sorrow, and ever-present consciousness of a support taken away" (Phelps xxii), and she retired from the Patapsco Female Institute and moved to Baltimore, Maryland. Almira warns her in the text *The Female Student: Lectures to Young Ladies on Female Education* that "All human beings must suffer pain and sorrow; but on a woman, do the evils, incident to human existence, fall within peculiar force.... How much of pain and sickness is the delicate frame of women called to endure?" (15).

Ever stoic, Almira suggests that "a truly good mother" is one "who can command her own feelings sufficiently to perform painful offices for the relief of those she loves, and even for the sake of common humanity" (232). Contrasting maternal agency with the figure of Niobe, who upon the death of her children turned to stone, Almira questions who "dissolved in sentimental grief, commiserates, without attempting to relieve?" (232). A mother's duty went beyond basic provision of needs for her children (Phelps 15). She must "elevate the minds of her offspring by frequent reference to a future state; she must teach them to hold the world and its pursuits in subservincy to more important interest, and to prize above all things that peace which, as the world giveth not, neither can it take away" (Phelps 15).

During her later years at Patapsco, Almira viewed herself as the "mother of nearly one hundred young girls," who knew that "her daughters must soon become actors (Phelps xvii). For Almira, the forecasting of women's agency was akin to the permeable boundaries evident in human maturity. She addressed her students, stating "You who are now before me, may in respect to age, be considered as children, older girls, and young ladies; yet we must admit this classification is not so distinctive as to render its application clear, in all cases—for here, as in the world of nature around us, the boundaries are not distinct lines, but one state gradually passes into another" (Phelps 167). Intellectual boundaries were similar. Almira contends the following: "You don't remember when you first began to think; that period is involved in as much mystery as the darkness of the grave. The dawning of the human intellect, like that of the natural day, is gradual and undefined." (Phelps 32) And sadly, like nature, was subject to degeneration: "It is the order of nature that maturity shall be followed by decay.... Nature herself seems to be growing old; the sun has risen upon many troublesome days and the moon has witnessed wearisome nights" (Phelps 32). Almira died on her birthday in 1884 at the age of ninety-one.

Almira could not have forecast the current environmental crisis, nor the scarcity of botany programs currently offered to students. Isabel Marques explains that the worldwide impact of declining botany programs may not yield enough graduates to replace those retiring, which is alarming because, according to her, botanical expertise is "fundamental to biodiversity, agricultural development, biofuel production, drug discovery and food science" (295). Her perspective is not unfounded. Others have pointed out that the field of botany has "experienced an absolute decline becoming nearly extinct" (Brint et al. 15) in current academic programs. The gradual extinction of a scientific field can be linked to the political ecology of education or, rather, the examination of "how political economic forces influence pedagogical opportunities" (Meek 2). Marques calls for an "engagement in outreach" to "devise fresh approaches to teaching upcoming generations about the importance of plants, relying less on pressed dead specimens" so that "public outreach bury botany's old-fashioned image once and for all" (295).

This "old fashioned image" is most likely due to the misogyny and dismissal faced by nineteenth-century female botanists. Pedagogically, Almira was advocating bringing students into the field and suggesting science lessons in general and botany in particular should not be "sedentary study" acquired "in the library" but rather should involve students looking "over the surface of the earth, along the banks of the winding brooks, on the borders of precipices, the sides of mountains and the depths of the forest" (Lincoln 14). Almira's perspective on botany parallels Jean Barr and Lynda Birke's equating "good science" with "responsible knowing" (133). "Good science" includes "feelings, acknowledges uncertainty, focuses on collective knowledge making, [and] creates links with communities outside the classroom walls" (101). Aspects of ecofeminism echo throughout Almira's texts. These tenets suggest that humans are not separate from or superior to the world but are rather part of a total ecology (Engelhardt). For Almira, complete knowledge of nature could never be "fully understood," and, thus, "the greatest Botanist ... must experience a feeling of humiliation" regarding an "ignorance of nature" (Lincoln 81). Botany was not "a trifling science"; it provided a way to "examine into the grand principles which it develops" and ultimately "into the working of Creative wisdom in one vast domain of nature" (Lincoln 81).

Almira expanded the margins set for nineteenth-century women and provided feminist science pedagogical innovations in botany that were buried for years. Ecofeminism challenges ideological assumptions and the hierarchical structure of power (Gaard 10), and such confrontations do not go implicitly and tacitly unheeded. Feminist research continues to face problems related to "de-legitimisation, especially on the grounds of supposed lack of objectivity, marginalisation from the main body of a discipline, and conceptual hostility when operating within the main body of a discipline" (Jenkins 266). A deep examination of the history of women in science implies more than Hendrick's suggestion regarding the provision of mere surveys of women's contribution to science (298), some of whom have been selected to the canon and others ignored. Biographer Bolzau writes of Almira that "An age is reflected in the lives of its people.... Probably no better illustration of this statement can be found than in the life of Almira Hart Lincoln Phelps, which reflects the changing conceptions of woman's sphere in the nineteenth century" (v). An investigation into women scientists who have been left unacknowledged not only brings lives out of the shadows but also, more importantly, plays a critical role in the naming of values and assumptions inherent to issues related to feminist science pedagogy and critical science literacy.

Feminist science pedagogy is concerned with not only the curriculum product but also the instructional means or how the content is taught. The role of a teacher facilitator is to empower students by encouraging them to "redefine the role science plays in their own lives" (Capobianco 2). Feminist science pedagogy entails employing texts that are "meaningful, malleable, and accessible to the everyday practitioner" (Capobianco 28). The historic disparagement of the "familiar" text designed to instruct all publics in scientific constructs today clouds transparency by relegating such science as only an avenue of popularization, which contributes to the politicization of science. During these critical times, when nature indeed seems "to be growing old" (Phelps 32), it is important that the academic enterprise remembers those women who instructed in what may be called citizen or civic science. If not, we lose the thread of how to conduct ourselves during perilous environmental times when the everyday of people's lives continue to be gravely affected. We can no longer fail to bring the public into the "science-politics interface," which, given the current global climate emergency, "can no longer be viewed as an exclusive domain for scientific experts and policy-makers only" (Backstrand 24). Remembering our roots as women and mothers represents the solitary component of environmental activism.

Almira describes the action of the creeping root, stating that it forces "its way perpendicularly into the earth, extends horizontally, and sends out fibres." She continues: "It is very tenacious of life.... This root is sometimes useful, by its fibres spreading and interlacing themselves, and thus rendering a soil more permanent" (54). Roots are not seen at "first glance," but upon "close examination and reflection," (12) they reveal important underpinnings. Remembering Almira's maternalist roots reveals her life to be one of contradiction, fraught with loss and a lack of acknowledgment. Bringing Almira's lessons to light was this author's attempt to bring back a past voice of science and maternalism into the current debate regarding preserving our children's place in the world. Despite Almira's roots growing in the shadow, they were "tenacious of life" and during one March morning, contributed to the foundation upon which Avery and I stood in the garden.

Works Cited

Abir-Am Pnina and Dorinda Outram. *Uneasy Careers and Intimate Lives Women in Science*. Rutgers, 1989.

Apparasu, Srinivasa Rao. "Telangana's 700-Year-Old Banyan Tree Gets Saline Drip for Survival." *Hindustan Times*, 19 Apr. 2018. www.hindustantimes.com/india-news/telangana-s-700-year-old-banyan-tree-gets-saline-drip-for-survival/story-ZvtuU2JFyJX71N mB5OhcbN.html. Accessed 28 May 2020.

Arnold, Barber, Lois. *Women's Education in the Nineteenth Century: Four Lives in Science.* Teachers College Press, 1982.

Barber, John Warner. *Connecticut Historical Collections, Containing a General Collection of Interesting facts, traditions, biographical Sketches, Anecdotes &c. Relating to the History and Antiquities of Every Town in Connecticut with Geographical Descriptions.* Published and Sold at New Haven, By John Barber and at Hartford, By Al. Willard. 1836.

Barnhart, John Hendly. "Some American Botanists of Former Days" *Torreya*, vol. 9, no. 12, Torrey Botanical Society, pp. 241-57.

Barr, Jean, and Lynda Birke. *Common Science? Women, science and knowledge.* Indiana University Press, 1998.

Bartlett, Ellen. "Emma Willard, Education for Women." *New England Magazine, An Illustrated Monthly*, vol. 25, American Company Publishers, Sept. 1901, pp. 555-76.

Beach, Alfred E. *Science Record for 1875. A Compendium of Scientific Progress and Discovery during the Past Year With Illustrations.* Munn & Company, 1875.

Bell, Susan Groag, and Marilyn Yalom. *Revealing Lives: Autobiography, Biography, and Gender.* SUNY Press, 1990.

Bollick, Margaret. "Women and plants in Nineteenth-Century American." *A Flowering of Quilts*, edited by Patricia Cox Crew, University of Nebraska Press, 2001, pp. 1-9.

Blackmore, Jill. *Educational Leadership and Nancy Fraser* Routledge, 2016.

Bolzau, Emma Lydia. *Almira Hart Lincoln Phelps: Her Life and Work.* Science Printing Company, 1936.

Brint, Steven, et al. "Declining Academic fields in U.S. Four Year Colleges and Universities 1970–2006." *Journal of Higher Education.* 2012, vol. 83, no. 4, pp. 582-613.

Browne, Janet. "Botany for Gentlemen: Erasmus Darwin and 'The Loves of the Plants.'" *Isis*, vol. 80, no. 4, pp. 593-621.

Capobianco, Brenda M. "Science Teachers' Attempts at Integrating Feminist Pedagogy through Collaborative Action Research". *Journal of Science Teaching*. vol. 44, no. 1, 2007, pp. 1-32.

Crosswhite, Frank S. and Carol D. Crosswhite. "The Plant Collecting Brandegees, with Emphasis on Katherine Brandegree as a Liberated Woman Scientist of Early California." *Desert Plant*. 1885, pp. 128-162.

Eldred, Janet Carey, and Peter Mortenson. "Almira Lincoln Phelps and the Composition of Democratic Teachers." *Imagining Rhetoric: Composing Women of the Early United States*, University of Pittsburg Press, 2002, pp. 145-188.

Englelhardt, Elizabeth, S. D. *The Tangled Roots of Feminism, Environmentalism and Appalachian Literature*. Ohio University Press, 2003.

Fara, Patricia. *Sex, Botany and Empire: The Story of Carl Linnaeus and Joseph Banks*. Columbia University Press, 2003.

Frank, Sally. "Eve Was Right to Eat the 'Apple': The Importance of Narrative in the Art of Lawyering," Yale Journal of Law & Feminism, vol. 8, no. 1, 1995, pp. 79-118.

Gagliano, Monica, et al. "Experience Teaches Plants to Learn Faster and Forget Slower in Environments Where It Matters." *Oecologia*, vol. 175, no. 1, 2014, pp. 63-72.

Gaard, G. *Ecofeminism: Women, Animals, Nature*. Temple University Press, 1993.

Gibson, Prudence, and Gagliano, Monica. "The Feminist Plant, Changing Relations with the Water Lily." *Ethics & the Environment*, vol. 22, no. 2, 2017, pp. 125-47.

Gianquitto, Tina. "Botany's Beautiful Arrangement: Almira Phelps and Enlightenment Science. *"Good Observers of Nature": American Women and the Scientific Study of the Natural World, 1820-1885*, University of Georgia Press, 2007, pp. 15-57.

Good, H. G. "Pennsylvania History: A Journal of Mid-Atlantic Studies." *Pennsylvania History: A Journal of Mid-Atlantic Studies*, vol. 3, no. 3, 1936, pp. 221-22.

Hale, Sarah Josepha Buell, and Henry Gardiner Adams. *A Cyclopaedia of Female Biography Consisting of Sketches of All Women Who Have Been Distinguished by Great Talents, Strength of Character, Piety,*

Benevolence, or Moral Virtue of Any Kind. Groombridge and Sons, 1857.

Hart, John Seely. "Almira Hart Lincoln Phelps" *The Female Prose Writers of America: with Portraits, Biographical Notices and Specimens of Their Writings.* E. H. Bulter and Co., 1857.

Head, Lesley, et al. "Vegetal Politics: Belonging, Practices and Places." *Social & Cultural Geography,* vol. 15 no. 8, 2014, pp. 861-70.

Hendrick, Robert. "Ever-widening Circle or Mask of Oppression?: Almira Phelps's Role in Nineteenth-century American Female Education, *History of Education,* vol. 24, no.4, 1995, pp. 293-304.

Jenkins, Katherine. "'That's Not Philosophy': Feminism, Academia and the Double Bind." *Journal of Gender Studies,* vol. 23, no. 3, Sept. 2014, pp. 262-74.

Kelley, Theresa M. *Clandestine Marriage: Botany and Romantic Culture.* John Hopkins University Press, 2012.

Keene, Melanie. "Familiar Science in Nineteenth Century Britain." *History of Science,* vol. 52, no. 1, 2014, pp. 53-71.

Keeney Elizabeth B. *The Botanizers: Amateur Scientists in Nineteenth-Century America.* The University of North Carolina Press, 1992.

Kohlstedt, Sally Gregory. "Parlors, Primers, and Public Schooling: Education for Science in Nineteenth-Century America." *Isis,* vol. 81, no. 3, 1990, pp. 424-45.

Kuiken, Vesna. *Active Enchantments: Form, Nature and Politics in American Literature.* Columbia University, 2015.

Larsen, Kristine. *The Women Who Popularized Geology in the 19th Century.* Springer Publishing, 2018.

LaFleur, Greta L. "Precipitous Sensations: Herman Mann's 'The Female Review' (1797), Botanical Sexuality, and the Challenge of Queer Historiography." *Early American Literature,* vol. 48, no. 1, 2013, pp. 93-123.

Lincoln, Almira H. *Familiar Lectures on Botany, Practical, Elementary and Physiological.* F. J. Huntington and Co., 1829.

Marder, Michael. "Plant Intentionality and the Phenomenological Framework of Plant Intelligence." *Plant Signaling & Behavior,* vol. 7, no. 11, pp. 1365-72.

McLeod, Kelly. "From Feminized Flora to Floral Feminism: Gender Representation and Botany." *New Mind's Eye*, 2015, newmindseye. wordpress.com/. Accessed 28 May 2020.

Marques, Isabel. "Teaching: Bury Botany's Outdated Image." *Nature*, April 2015.

Meek, David. "Toward a Political Ecology of Education: The Educational Politics of Scale in Southern Para Brazil." *Environmental Education Research*, vol. 21, no. 3, 2014, pp. 447-59.

North, Catherine Melinda. *History of Berlin, Connecticut*. The Tuttle Morehous & Taylor Co., 1915.

Phelps, Mrs. *Botany for Beginners: Introduction to Mrs. Lincoln's Lectures on Botany for the Use of Common Schools and the Younger Pupils of Higher Schools and Academies*. Huntington and Savage, 1849.

Phelps, Mrs. Lincoln. *The Educator: Or Hours with My Pupils*. A. S. Barnes & Company, 1876.

Rossiter, Margaret W. *Women Scientists in America: Struggles and Strategies to 1940*. The Johns Hopkins Press, 1982.

Rudolph, Emanuel D. "Almira Lincoln Phelps (1793-1884) and the Spread of Botany in Nineteenth Century America." *American Journal of Botany*, vol. 71, no. 8, 1984, pp. 1161-67.

Ryan, John Charles. "The Botanical Imagination." *Plants in Contemporary Poetry: Ecocriticism and the Botanical Imagination*, Routledge Press, 2018, pp. 1-26.

Sewall, Richard Benson. "Schooling" *The Life of Emily Dickinson*, Harvard University Press, Cambridge, 1980, pp. 335-67.

Scott, Ann Firor. "Almira Lincoln Phelps: The Self-Made Woman in the Nineteenth Century." *Making the Invisible Woman Visible*. University of Illinois Press, 1984, pp. 89-106.

Shteir, Ann B. *Cultivating Women, Cultivating Science: Flora's Daughters and Botany in England*. John Hopkins University Press, 1996.

Sundberg, Marshall D. "Botanical education in the United States: Part 2, The Nineteenth Century—Botany for the Masses vs. the Professionalization of Botany." *Plant Science Bulletin*, vol. 58, no. 3, 2012, pp. 101-31.

Taiz, Lincoln, and Lee Taiz. *Flora Unveiled: The Discovery and Denial of Sex in Plants*. Oxford University Press, 2017.

Teute, Fredrika J. "The Loves of Plants; Or, the Cross-Fertilization of Science and Desire at the End of the Eighteenth Century" *Huntington Library Quarterly*, vol. 63, no. 3, 2000, pp. 319-345.

Thurs, Daniel Patrick. *Science in Popular Culture: Contested Meanings and Cultural Authority in American.* University of Wisconsin. 2004.

Tolley, Kim. *The Science Education of American Girls: A Historical Perspective.* Routledge Press, 2003.

Van der Veen, Marijke. "The Materiality of Plants: Plant-People Entanglements." *World Archaeology*, vol. 46, no. 5, Dec. 2014, pp. 799-812.

Zaraska, Marta. "Smarty Plants" *Discover*, vol. 38, no. 4, May 2017, pp. 52-57.

Mother Earth

Andromeda Bromwich

Chapter Four

Access to Healthy and Clean Food in Turkey: Food Activism and Mothers' Concerns about Shopping for Change

Nurcan Atalan-Helicke

Food retains a central importance in family life and represents an expression of love (Bellows, Alcaraz, and Hallman). Although the work of feeding the family is invisible as work, it is central to the construction of family and femininity (DeVault). Food work involves all of the labour that goes into procuring and preparing food (e.g., shopping for ingredients, cooking, and cleaning up) as well as the mental and emotional labour of planning meals and addressing health needs (e.g., nutrition and food allergies) (Cairns and Johnston). Food studies literature has discussed consumer shopping behaviour for alternative food and demonstrates how different considerations and ethics often conflict and create tension and anxieties, particularly for the Northern consumer (Fuentes and Fuentes; Meah and Watson; Wilkerson). Food activism in the Global North can involve becoming locavores, vegetarians, vegans, or organic moms; rallying against the safety and corporate control of genetically modified (GM) food; and demanding, through petitions, that food industry change their be-haviour. Food activism has become a symbol of modern politics (Gray). The factors that rally food activists for so-called healthy and good food are complex and interrelated, such as sustainability ethics, hunger, household budget, culture, sensory preferences, convenience, and health status (Anderson; Cairns and Johnston; Schaefer et al.). Food activism highlights how citizenship, responsibility, and social justice interact with consumerism in society, individual decision making, and broad changes in the agricultural and food (agrifood) system in new and complex ways. However, examples of food activism in the Global North, and how it imagines changing the agrifood system, may not capture the possibilities and limitations in a country in the Global South. Here, I address this gap with a case study of mothers and their food activism in the context of Turkey.

The June 2011 cover of a magazine in Turkey—which was published by an Islamic food security organization[1] working on access to clean food—urged mothers to "feed halal food to their children to protect them" (GIMDES). The cover of the magazine published by the Association for the Inspection and Certification of Food and Supplies (Gıda ve Ihtiyaç Maddeleri Denetleme ve Sertifikalandırma Derneği or GIMDES) did not specify what children need to be protected from. However, the articles in the magazine discussed the importance of "clean" and "healthy" food and, particularly, why mothers should avoid GM food while feeding their children, which the organization defined as not clean and halal. Halal is an Arabic word meaning "lawful" or "permitted" according to Islamic principles. It signifies "pure" and "healthy" and provides certain basic principles to follow in everyday practices of Muslims (Atalan-Helicke; Fischer). GIMDES is a nonprofit organization spearheading the institutionalization of halal certification in Turkey. Since 2011, GIMDES has also organized several workshops to educate women, particularly mothers, to choose halal and non-genetically modified food to be healthy and to raise a healthy generation.

Not long after, in February 2012, the Internet site of a national secular television station in Turkey reported about a group of mothers in Eskişehir, a city of a million people in central Turkey, where I grew up, who set up an organic food distribution network connecting producers to consumers. The story praised these mothers as powerful as "one thousand tigers" (Sert). The story continued with details on how these mothers directly sought and connected to organic farmers to access food clean of genetically modified organisms (GMOs). The reporter, who is a mother herself, wrote: "I thought mothers were divided into two.

Those who are dedicated to not allowing their child(ren) to eat one gram of pesticides no matter what, and those who do not care because children would eat [contaminated food] at daycare anyway. I was wrong. There is a third category of mothers. Those who think about not only what families eat today but also what they will eat tomorrow" (Sert). The story's language about "moms on a mission" and its focus on mothering and feeding the family as well as the protecting children and future generations through food consumption highlight the intersectionality of the anti-GMO movement and consumer activism with motherhood. The same month, Greenpeace Turkey, the national branch of the international environmental organization, started its "We Won't Eat" anti-GM campaign. Although gender was not a theme for Greenpeace Turkey in its campaign to revert the decision to import GM animal feed (Tüsev), its anti-GM movement used images of women as mothers as well as children across the campaign, especially one with mothers and their kids protesting buying milk from animals that are fed with GM animal feed.

What is common in the demands of these anti-GM campaigns, consumer food access groups, and education efforts? They emerged in the aftermath of Turkey's Biosafety Commission's decision in 2011 to import three genetically modified soy varieties and eleven GM corn varieties as animal feed. They involve urban, middle-class consumers who can access the Internet,[2] and they target mothers, who are seen as responsible for feeding their family healthy food and as guardians of health and morality in the family (Parsons; Marshall). To some extent, Turkish mothers have internalized norms of "intensive mothering" (Hays)—a child-centered, expert-guided, and labour-intensive parenting style that emphasizes the devotion of mothers. The messages of anti-GM campaign nourish both acknowledged and latent anxieties in a risk society and destabilize the feeling of safety among mothers (Beck). Although they point to growing concerns about a global and industrialized food system, in which an increasing number of food additives, synthetic ingredients and harmful chemicals, and production practices contaminate food, they do not address the dilemmas mothers face to meet contemporary standards for being a good mother, a healthy woman, a discerning consumer, and an ethically minded shopper making a change in the food system with their choices.

In what follows, I examine the concerns of mothers about accessing clean and healthy food in a developing country fully integrated into globalized agrifood system[3] and how they negotiate their food choices and shop in alternative food markets as a form of resistance to the mainstream food system and as a form of activism. Studies have focused on mothers and consumers in the Global North and on how women express their agency in different forms individually or collectively to promote good food, to demonstrate their dissatisfaction with the price or quality of food, and to pressure the state and markets to reflect their values in food production and distribution. These case studies include mothers' activism, food shopping behaviour, and food related anxieties in Italy (Counihan), the United States (Afflerback et al.; Bellows, Alcaraz, and Hallman), francophone Europe (Pasche Guignard), Sweden (Anving and Sellerberg), and Canada (Cairns et al.), among others. Although they point to the success of women's food activism throughout history—such as the consumer boycotts in 1920s and 1940s in urban and rural America when working women and housewives established alliances and used motherhood to voice their complaints publicly (Stolle and Micheletti)—these studies have mainly focused on and critically engaged with the notions and ideals of "reflexive consumer," "conscious consumption," "eco-moms," and "sustainable family" that emerged and coincided with neoliberal economies after the 1990s (Cairns et al.; Johnston and Szabo; Pasche Guignard). Even though there are studies about food anxieties of consumers in the developing countries, such as Brazil and Uganda, they are often associated with food insecurity and the challenges concerning how to address imminent and chronic food shortages (Bohn and Veiga; Kyomugisha et al.). Thus, the concerns of mothers in the developing world or the Global South are assumed to be different from those in the Global North (Jackson). Also, an exclusive focus on Northern consumers and their ethical consumption "continues to locate consumption within a Northern-centric global imaginary" and prevents recognition of the actualities and possibilities of ethical consumption in the Global South (Gregson and Ferdous, 253).

I examine Turkish mothers' engagement in alternative food markets through three questions. What are the concerns of mothers in Turkey about clean and healthy food? How do they engage with alternative food markets to access and seek GM-free food? What are the tensions in mothers' expectations of and experiences with these alternative food markets and the limitations of shopping for change? I argue that urban middle-class mothers in the Global South share similar anxieties with those in the Global North, such as the use of pesticides and GM food in feeding their families. Mothers' anxieties about the food system point to the changing role of the state in regulating and monitoring food delivery as well as to the limitations of alternative food markets to deliver consumer expectations about clean and healthy food. In these neoliberal times, during which governments have delegated responsibility for health, wellbeing, and happiness onto self-regulating individuals, Turkish mothers have become increasingly under the surveillance of the state as well as business and civil society organizations; their lifestyles, particularly how they feed their families, have been disciplined. Even middle- to high-class consumer women negotiate their environmentally sensitive choices with their financial and time constraints. Moreover, structural challenges, such as lack of labelling for genetically modified food, limit the effect of mothers' food choices.

Food Activism as Environmental Activism

Sustainable consumption, and particularly sustainable food consumption, has become an important form of environmental activism. Studies about Northern activists have shown that consumers have different motivations for becoming involved in the food movement (Allen and Sachs) and have rallied around various topics, including the environment, animal welfare, health concerns, human rights, and fighting inequality (Alkon and Agyeman). Proponents of food activism argue that ecological citizenship expressed through consumer behaviour for local, organic, fair trade, or GM-free food can save the world and transform market practices (Seyfang). There is broad consensus that consumers are key actors to bring about change (Johnston and Szabo) and that sustainable food choices are good not only for the consumer but also for the future of ecosystems (Johnston et al.)

Women participate in food movements in several ways: as producers, consumers, and activists within social movements. Research shows that women in the Global North are still responsible for the majority of food-related work (e.g., food purchasing, planning, preparing, and cleaning up), but they control few resources and do not hold much decision-making power in the food industry (Cairns and Johnston). Similarly, it is typically middle-class white men who dominate food movements in the Global North (Allen and Sachs).[4] Although different studies have examined gendered food preferences and eating (Avakian and Haber; Parasecoli), specific reasons for these differences are not easily identified due to social and cultural differences among groups and individuals. Yet some studies argue that the females' involvement of food activities starting in early childhood (compared to males) as well as their more direct and knowledgeable contact with food were further enhanced by the traditional roles of motherhood and family caregiving (Caraher et al.; Furst et al.), and these practices, habits and expectations affect their sustainable consumption practices. In terms of gender differences in sustainable food consumption, general wisdom is that "highly educated young mothers with children from higher income and partnered households form the most important consumer group for organic and healthy foods" in the Global North (Bellows, Alcaraz, and Hallman 548). Yet Ann Bellows and her colleagues' study about consumer preferences for organic, local and GM-free food in the United States found no significant difference among female and male preferences for organic food, whereas GM-free food preference was highest among female consumers.

Consumers', and mainly mothers', desire for clean and healthy food also stem from broader narratives about obesity as an epidemic and risk to the current and future health of the society (Cairns and Johnston). Mothers are particularly singled out in obesity discourse as responsible for the body size of their children (McNaughton). By presenting obesity as a serious health threat of epidemic proportions, experts, health professionals, and even media celebrities make individual women scapegoats for broader problems in the agrifood systems and introduce new forms of governance for surveillance and control of the bodies and lifestyles of women (Mansfield). Studies about mothering and feeding also demonstrate how women's bodies become subject to judgment "from womb to tomb" and women become more concerned about the healthy eating of their girls than their boys so that they will not become fat (McNaughton). While mothers negotiate the pleasures and anxieties of food, they seek external sources of information and advice on how to mother appropriately, which are often consistent with the ideology of intensive mothering (Afflerback et al.; Hays). In the mothers' quest, paediatricians and health professionals with formal qualifications provide authoritative information, but they are not the only source that mothers take their advice from. Celebrity chefs, public pedagogues, and moral entrepreneurs have risen to increasing prominence in recent years and provide culinary guidance and lifestyle advice; they aim to address alleged deficits in consumer knowledge (Jackson). Mothers also receive advice from the Internet, parenting magazines, and books, and they look for authoritative knowledge to help them become a so-called good mother, which, overall, contributes to increasing food anxieties and makes food choices more complex.

Although consumer-based activity is recognized as an important source of environmental and social change, the limitations of consumer-based forms of food activism in the Global North are also acknowledged. Some suggest that seemingly progressive initiatives may mask processes and ideologies of neoliberalism, in which state responsibility for food safety and food security are delegated to self-regulating individuals (Allen et al.; Guthman, "Neoliberalism"). Other critiques discuss the privileges embedded in the alternative food markets and the failure of alternative food movements to recognize the exclusiveness of organic products or local farmers' markets (Guthman, "Fast Food/Organic Food"; DuPuis, Lindsey Harrison, and Goodman). Similar critiques are raised in terms of anti-GM campaigns and labelling movements that emphasize shopping for GM-free food and consumer rights to choose yet fail to address GM food regulation (Roff). Studies also discuss the co-optation of the alternative food markets—such as pushing small producers out of the organic market in the Global North (Guthman, "Agrarian Dreams") and the mainstreaming of the Fairtrade system (Jaffee)—to exemplify that alternative food markets are not immune to the conventional logic of industrial production (Le Velly and Dufeu). Thus, food activists emphasize the need for a multiracial and multiclass alternative food movement, which could open up new possibilities (Alkon and Guthman).

Although these debates have been productive, they have also created binaries between ecological citizens working for the collective good and self-maximizing consumers (Cairns and Johnston), between local and global food, and between alternative versus conventional food networks (Le Velly and Dufeu). Studies now argue for a more nuanced understanding of the citizen-consumer hybrid (Johnston) and to incorporate the value of ethical consumption as one of the tools and actions available for people and groups to make social change (Willis and Schor). Scholars highlighting the intersection of food and femininities also argue for a nuanced approach to women's engagement with alternative food markets (Cairns and Johnston). Mothers' shopping at organic markets to feed their families sustainable food has been criticized as a form of intensive mothering among middle-class consumers in the United States and Canada (Cairns et al.). Yet "such critiques can work to dismiss women's politicized food work" and can deny "the political significance of wo-men's social reproductive work in the realm of home and family" (Cairns and Johnston 38). Kate Cairns and Josée Johnston argue that approaching "ethical consumption not as a form of care but as a form of gendered care work" (37) also provides an opportunity to understand the contradictions and emotions attached to food shopping and its implications for gender roles. The following case study of Turkey shows that although consumers in the Global South share similar anxieties about the food system, their engagement with alternative food markets are more nuanced due to changes in the agrifood system, the emergence of hybrid structures of alternative food markets, the complex identities of the consumers, and the relationship of consumers to the political systems and the state.

Methodology

Fifty-six mothers across nine focus groups discussed their food prac-tices and perspectives on family meals in Ankara, the capital city of Turkey, and in Konya, a highly urbanized city in central Turkey, in the summer of 2015.[3] The cities share similar characteristics. Women in both cities have access to farmers markets, supermarkets, organic, and halal markets. Both cities provide employment opportunities for women outside the home. Konya is often characterized as the capital city of the Islamic bourgeoisie in Turkey (Mumyakmaz).

The participants in the focus groups also completed a survey about their age, socioeconomic status, education and marital status, household shopping practices (e.g., local, organic, and halal preferences), food budgets, their sources of information on healthy food, and what types of food they prepare from scratch at home.

The focus groups were carried out in the participants' homes and daycare centres. Childcare was provided during the focus groups. The participants were recruited via word of mouth through key informants and posts on online mothering groups. Their diversity in terms of age and religious values allowed participants to share individual and collective anxieties and concerns, regardless whether they were secular or Muslim.[5] The conversations also elicited emotional responses—a reflection of not only food's emotional salience in everyday lives (Cairns and Johnston), but also of the cultural and political polarization between the secular and the Muslim groups in Turkey. (Tuğal) Two fathers accompanied their wives to the focus groups, and they participated in the discussions. Although the men's responses were recorded, only the women participants' accounts were included in the data analysis (Table 1).

The youngest research participant was twenty-seven years old, and the oldest was sixty-four; 84 per cent (n=48) of the participants had children under the age of 18 living in the same house. Only one of the respondents was divorced, and she lived with her parents. She was taking care of her daughter, parents, and unemployed brother at the time of the study. None of the women in the research group defined themselves as overweight or fat.

The participants were mainly middle class, who had a high level of education; the majority of participants (61 per cent) had an undergraduate degree or more. Their high educational attainment is also reflected in the higher incomes of the participants: almost half of the participants (n=24) were in a high income bracket and had monthly household incomes of more than 4,000 Turkish liras (1,520 USD) (Table 2). The high household incomes can also be attributed to the occupational identities of the participants: almost 60 per cent of the women (n=33) had a fulltime occupation outside the home. Four participants were retired, whereas nineteen defined themselves as housewives.

Agrifood System Changes in Turkey

Turkey is going through a nutrition transition associated with Westernization of diets, changes in socioeconomic levels, global integration, and urbanization, which is similar to other countries in the Middle East (Pingali; Popkin Adair, and Ng). The nutrition transition has often led to an emergence of hybrid diets and dishes, and these new diets consist of imported products and traditional foods (Sodjinou et al.; Désilets et al.) Studies suggest an increasing risk of chronic diseases associated with lifestyles and dietary changes in countries undergoing a nutrition transition, where the incidence of infectious diseases declines and chronic diseases emerge as a major cause of morbidity and mortality (Fleischer et al.). Concerns about the effects of nutrition transition, such as obesity, thus dominate media stories and public health researchers in Turkey. Some scholars and groups, such as GIMDES, have been distressed about these forms of western imperialism in terms of food, as reflected in the rise of the number of global fast food chains and supermarkets in Turkish cities. These groups have also warned about the invisible risks associated with the environmental, chemical, and medical threats associated with modernity that could affect the body and the mind (Büyüközer). With the lengthening of the food supply chain, the increasing of food imports, the introduction of synthetic ingredients in food, and news stories about scandals related to tainted food, consumers have also become subject to shifting nutritional advice (Büyüközer; Karatay). Changes in body size and associated concerns about chronic diseases caused the Ministry of Health to initiate an obesity public health plan in 2010, which it would update every five years with data about nutrition, the recommended amount of physical activity for different age groups, and specific targets about healthy nutrition (Sağlık Bakanlığı).

Turkey is a middle-income country and well integrated into global markets. It is a top producer and exporter of wheat, high-value fruits, and vegetables to other Muslim-majority countries in the Middle East and Central Asia as well as countries in the European Union with large Muslim populations (OECD). The share of small producers has declined sharply since 2001 due to Turkey's integration into global and regional markets as well as to the World Bank Agricultural Reform Implementation Program (Adaman, Karapınar, and Ozertan). Consumers have also observed the consolidation of food distribution networks and supermarket chains over the last two decades. Legal changes, such as the Seed Law, and market regulations have made it difficult for small producers to compete against big producers (Atasoy; Atalan-Helicke and Mansfield). Yet consumers always have had access to farmers markets and fresh produce outside of the conventional supermarket distribution system.

Local farmers markets have always been available in neighbourhoods, connecting conventional produce to urban consumers with outdoor markets established every week in the same location. Although it is middlemen who sell the produce at these local markets, consumers often have a chance to establish trust with the seller and learn about where the food comes from. Sometimes the producers can market their produce directly to the consumer by bringing their produce in small vans to different neighbourhoods, but not on a set schedule. Since 2006, some cities have also established organic farmers' markets. However, organic outdoor farmers' markets are limited in number and not widely accessible to every consumer.

Organic production in Turkey has been growing since 1980 as a result of demand for organic food in the European markets rather than from grassroots consumer demand[6] (Ataseven and Gunes; ETO). As of 2019, there are 213 organically certified crops grown by about 53,000 registered organic farmers on 386,000 hectares of land. There are 249 registered farmers who raise organic livestock. Organic figs, hazelnuts, apricots, and wheat are some of the top exported commodities to European and American markets (Tarım Orman). Although domestic consumption of organic food is increasing, particularly due to aspirations of urban consumers to lead a healthy life as well as anxiety over the health of their children, it is mainly environmentally conscious, middle- to high-income consumers that consume organic food in Turkey (Eryılmaz et al). Because organic food is more expensive, and the price fluctuates from crop to crop during time, even high- to middle-income consumers are sensitive to the high cost of organic food in Turkey. (Kenanoğlu Bektaş and Karahan Uysal) Consumers in general also worry about the regulation and enforcement of organic standards in organic markets (Sarıkaya), which are similar to consumer worries about the monitoring of food safety, the lengthening of food supply and the lack of labelling of GM food in Turkey.

GM crops become ingredients in hundreds of food products that humans consume, and without proper labelling requirements on imported food, it raises questions for consumers (Atalan-Helicke). Turkey does not produce GM crops, but it has imported GM soy and maize as animal feed since 2011. It also imports food products from countries that have GM agriculture. An anti-GM movement led by an umbrella organization of secular groups has been active in Turkey since Turkey's ratification of the Cartagena Protocol in 2004. Muslims in Turkey have also been active in the GM food debates in Turkey over the past decade and have published several popular books on the intersection of halal and GM food (Buyukozer; Ozer). However, the complexity of defining GM food from an Islamic perspective leads to multiple interpretations of the halal status of GM food (Atalan-Helicke).

In one of the most comprehensive studies about consumer attitudes towards GM food, Özdemir Oğuz found that 60 per cent of Turkish consumers perceived GM food to be a great risk to both human and environmental health. Based on the findings from face-to-face interviews with 2,431 individuals, both men and women, from different regions, age groups, as well as education and economic groups, the study found that one-third of participants rejected the idea that GM agriculture was more profitable for Turkey. The study found that the participants with higher educational levels were less likely to find GM acceptable than those at a lower educational level. Despite these concerns, Oguz's study also found low levels of awareness about GM food and emphasized the importance of providing the Turkish population with information about GM food. Low levels of knowledge about GM food but high levels of risk perception are also among the key findings in another study carried out with low- and middle-income mothers in Erzurum in Eastern Turkey (Öztürk, Şahin, and Tüfekçi). Based on the findings of surveys carried out with 397 mothers with infants under the age of one, Sibel Öztürk and colleagues found that majority of mothers learned about GM food on television. Although the mothers did not think industrial or processed packaged food, such as powdered soup mixes or biscuits, had GM ingredients, they defined GM food as harmful to human health.

Mothers' fears about food safety and ingredients also stem from the media in Turkey, which has increasingly highlighted the carcinogenic ingredients found in processed food or GM organism traces in baby food (Kadak; "Ünlü"). Thus, responding to and negotiating risk has become a dominant aspect of life for consumers feeding themselves and their families in Turkey. Although these scandals can be attributed to the lack of enforcement and monitoring by the Turkish state, they also emerge at a period when the Turkish Ministry of Food, Agriculture, and Livestock has increased enforcement and monitoring of food safety and quality by harmonizing its legislation with the European Union. These harmonization efforts included the adaptation of food directives on contaminants, food safety, and hygiene by vertically and horizontally harmonizing Turkish Food Codex with the new regulations and expanding the requirement of Hazard Analysis and Critical Control Points (HACCP) in food production facilities to prevent biological, chemical, and physical hazards in the food production processes (USDA

GAIN). Indeed, the Ministry of Agriculture, Food, and Livestock reported that between 2016 and 2017, it found GM traces over the legally defined threshold of GMO content of 0.9 per cent but rejected less than one per cent (0.95 per cent) of all checked imported food ("Bakan"). In the analysis that follows, I discuss how Turkish mothers perceive the risks in the agrifood system and what kind of factors affect their choices of finding clean and healthy food.

Findings

Heavy Burdens: Food System Changes and Growing Concerns

When asked what they pay attention to when choosing food, several participants stated that they were careful about ingredients of the food as well as how it was produced. Filiz[7] mentioned that she spends a lot of time reading the labels in the supermarket: "I read the ingredients ... not just whether it has sugar, milk, but also additives and preservatives." The sentiment about chemical residues in the food and their connection to disease was a common concern among several participants in different focus groups. They raised concerns about the health effects of changes in the food system, problems in regulation and monitoring of food, as well as disagreements about the long-term health impacts of different ingredients in food. Women discussed several issues, including but not limited to, the link between agricultural chemical residues and disease; the impact of hormones and food additives on obesity and early menarche; uncertainty about the health impacts of GM animal feed and industrially processed food ingredients; and the link between food ingredients and allergies.

Referring to the changing patterns of agricultural production and the lengthening of food supply chain, Zelha said, "We hear so many things about how it is not possible to produce vegetables without chemicals." Several participants also talked about the availability of vegetables year round. Although some were happy about the convenience, others were suspicious about the long-term health impacts of growing food in winter. Fulya said as follows: "I bought some tomatoes in the winter and their seeds have started to grow inside the tomato by themselves. Are these growth hormones? What will they do in your body?"

Whereas it was common knowledge to wash vegetables in water mixed with vinegar to clean them from contaminants causing gastrointestinal disease, several participants mentioned the difficulty of knowing about all chemicals and learning to get rid of them in their own kitchen. Betul mentioned that "Some agricultural chemicals are so strong. I wash all the vegetables [that I prepare] in vinegar water. But I heard that vinegar water doesn't wash away these new chemicals. I heard these chemicals cause cancer." Deniz responded with sarcasm and said "Everything makes cancer nowadays." Deniz said that she reads every food label in the supermarket because her husband had cancer. She was also frustrated because he had "been very careful about his lifestyle all his life." She also shared that she felt stressed: "I buy only organic food. I pay extra attention to food. I feel that food is the only thing I can control when everything around us is carcinogenic." Although Deniz's remarks about her stress on feeding her family and shopping for organic food reflect her maternal care and selflessness along the norms of intensive mothering (Cairn et al.), her concerns also stem from the widespread use of chemicals in the industrial food chain and, particularly, the extensive increase of pesticide use in Turkey (Delen et al.).

Almost all mothers knew about GM food. Whereas some read about GMOs in the newspapers, National Geographic, and ecological magazines, Fulya said she teaches about them at the middle school she works. Several mothers mentioned avoiding GM food for health reasons. While studies have not been conclusive about their health impacts,[8] Irem mentioned her daughter's allergies and their link to consuming GM food:

> My daughter has several allergies. The doctors could not figure it out for many years. She is allergic to anything that contains soy as well as red fruits, exotic food items like chocolate and coconut. You know, allergy is a rich person's disease. We buy only one brand of milk because if the cows eat GM soybeans, then she definitely has flare ups. We buy [raw] milk, and my mom makes the yoghurt for us. I cannot trust the yoghurt in the market.

Whereas Irem was the most knowledgeable and concerned about secondary effects of consuming GM food, others also had their own lists of food to avoid. Nursen also shared the strict diet she follows for her daughter who has egg and milk allergies: "When she became a toddler and her allergies became clear, her doctor suggested that we eliminate chicken from her diet to see whether we could control her allergies. I did not know chickens consume so many allergens. Then I heard [that] chicken eat GM animal feed." Participants' remarks about medical advice and safety of GM food demonstrate how women get their information and whom they choose to trust amid all the "misinformation and myths about GM food" as summed up by Esra.

Several participants mentioned talking to other women face to face or on social media about their food choices and learning from them. Melda mentioned about sharing the information she learns about good food on social media, but she also cautioned about "all the manipulated information on the Internet about GM food." She said she prefers to read "academically written research" because "sometimes agricultural engineers write that GM food is not harmful, and they also blame the public for worrying about GMOs for the wrong reasons." Melda's remarks are similar to concerns raised by anti-GM activism in the Global North and the South, where the topic of GM food becomes "scientized," which grants experts a high level of political authority and narrowing of opportunities for participation of ordinary citizens in the debate (Kinchy). Participants' use of the Internet to learn about and share information on the Internet also raises interesting questions about activism and social media campaigns in the current era.

Nihan mentioned receiving emails from the Greenpeace Turkey campaign on social media, but she was hesitant "to participate in the petition campaign." Nihan was vague about the reasons for not participating in a campaign emphasizing lifestyle changes (not shopping for food contaminated with GM), but her focus group participants discussed the implications of this campaign on political change and how demanding the Turkish state to label GM food and enforce regulation could be perceived as a structural change. Discussing the divide between the secular and Islamic organizations in their anti-GM campaigns, three focus group participants then talked about their fear of the real intentions of such groups and how such organizations as Greenpeace Turkey could manipulate a food safety issue as a political problem. Although they were aware of GIMDES's warnings about GM food and its suggestions for eating halal food to avoid GM food, they were concerned that their affiliation with the environmental campaign could be seen as criticism of the current government of Turkey. Esra acknowledged that "Greenpeace [Turkey] is a leftist organization, and they never work with our groups," referring to their lack of campaigns involving Islamic organizations and their lack of effort catering to devout Muslim consumers like her. Although she was concerned about the divide among the secular and Islamic organizations, as well as groups, she said she was also hopeful. She added that "maybe women could work together" and that "working for clean [anti-GM] food" with a diverse range of groups could "make the state and the markets deliver clean and healthy food." Esra's remarks, along with Melda's, demonstrate that research participants did not perceive the anti-GM campaign as a lifestyle change but rather as a broader structural food system problem requiring the state's involvement.

Healthy Choices and Shopping for Alternative Food

In their quest for healthy and clean food, women reported different options. Although some got their produce directly from the farmers through relatives and word of mouth, a few chose to shop from the same vendor in their pazar, or weekly neighborhood market. Some mentioned that a few supermarkets started labelling the origin (e.g., the city) where the food was sourced from. This labeling has made some of the particiants feel more connected to local food, whereas others sought only certified organic or certified halal products.

Whereas Filiz said she would shop only at supermarkets "to avoid unregulated processed food," Ajda said she would not trust big markets and buy only from small producers: "Do you know the small trucks that come to your neighborhoods? I have a few vendors whom I trust, and I know where they bring their vegetables from. The tomatoes may not be all shiny and round, but I believe they are natural." The emphasis on natural food often led to heated conversations, since the women all looked for different markers—such as natural look, taste, and good smell—in their quest for clean and healthy food. However, like other countries in the Global North, the term "natural" is not regulated in Turkey. Similar tensions emerged in mothers' definitions of organic and halal food, and how they contextualized it in relation to certification.

Local Food

In the Turkish context, when women refer to local food, they refer to the traceability of the food to a certain geographical region, regardless of the distance it travelled to their kitchen. Whereas sourcing food from a producer provides access to more natural food, several participants also reported that they trust local food because it would have fewer chemicals and would less likely arrive adulterated. Although all of the women were urban, several women reported having relatives in a rural area who provided them with their vegetables, pulses, and dried fruits. Ozum received her family's vegetables from her husband's aunt, who started her own garden after retiring in Antalya, a city on the Mediterranean coast that can grow vegetables year round. Ozum said she could receive "fresh food" through biweekly shipments. Almost half the women reported that they sourced their olive oil directly from the Aegean coast, which is the main area of olive oil production in Turkey, regardless of whether or not their family was from that region.

When Sozsel talked about the "advantages of living in Konya," she mentioned having "easy access to natural yoghurt and free-range chicken." Her parents have a garden on the outskirts of Konya and send her family tomatoes and vegetables all summer. She mentioned that living in Konya "means living in a natural environment with easy access to healthy food." However, Sozsel's remarks about "easy access to healthy food" revealed differences in terms of access between locals and outsiders. Eysen, who had moved to Konya for work, complained that her family is not from Konya and she does not have access to local or natural food that the other participants mentioned: "The access [Sozsel] mentioned only works for those who are from Konya. It is a privilege." The emphasis on privilege of access to local food emerged in two other focus groups in terms of being well connected to local vendors and having time to seek local food. Time and privilege also dominated conversations about access to private gardens. Four participants had their own gardens in their houses or plots they rented in urban farms and produced their vegetables in the summer. One participant grew tomatoes on her balcony downtown "as natural as possible, to the extent allowed by the chemicals of the city's air pollution." Although access to land and even a balcony to grow food was accepted as a privilege, some participants also acknowledged it as a way to resist the expansion of urban boundaries and cityscapes and not to lose the connection to the land.

For women who did not have access to relatives or "well-known vendors in the places were good food is grown" as Ayse put it, online natural food groups came handy. Eight participants had ordered food through these Internet groups or directly from a natural/organic farm with online order system, such as the one established by groups of mothers in Eskisehir.[9] Gul said she is happy to receive her food box through the email distribution system because she knows that producers in the internet group "follow good agricultural practices." However, these self-reported forms of quality control were not adequate for some women to trust these alternative food networks. Hayriye was concerned about monitoring the practices of local producers within the distribution system by other sellers and through consumer feedback. Two others mentioned that even though the online natural food groups they follow are self-monitored, and follow participatory guarantee systems, they still had concerns about a few vendors and their natural products. These remarks reflect the participants' doubts about the capacity of the markets and self-made food groups to deliver their values without proper enforcement and reporting to a separate organization (or the state).

When Canan mentioned how certain supermarkets started putting the place of origin for their produce and meat items, others protested whether that counts as "local food." Canan shared that based on her geographical knowledge, she tries "to follow seasonality and match local produce to naturalness." Gul's concerns were more focused on the inputs in agrifood systems: "We used to have a seasonal vacation house outside Ankara. We would spend weekends there and cultivate our garden. In the past, when the tomato seeds fell, they would produce again the next year. They do not anymore. I don't think local producers pay attention to what kind of seeds they use." The concern about the changes in the agricultural inputs was also shared by Aysin and Hatice. Hatice challenged the assumption that villages are more natural and that sourcing food from a local producer guarantees better food. She added that her grandmother "still lives in her village but everyone in her village buys eggs from the store. Nobody has chicken. [They] collected all the chicken." She was referring to the bird flu outbreak at the end of 2006 and the state authorities' decision to collect and slaughter two and half million poultry. This crisis led to the consolidation of the poultry industry in Turkey (Sarnıç). Hatice continued her remarks with a focus on sugar and food additives:

> When the villagers make jams, they also use the same sugar we buy from the markets. They may also use preservatives to extend shelf life. They give the same animal feed to their animals sold at the markets. They use the same hormones on their livestock. They feed their livestock GM animal feed. They also have to produce things cheap ... to make a living.

Hatice's remarks about the livelihoods and choices of farmers resemble other participants' statements on the increasing poverty of small producers, their lack of competitiveness against supermarkets, the rising popularity of contract farming in relation to local food, and the broader agrifood system changes in Turkey. Her remarks also demonstrate that as a consumer, she was aware of the limits of her shopping. Although she could help the businesses around her through shopping for alternative food, she was also aware of the structural problems that prevent a wider availability of nonindustrial and small-scale production in Turkey.

Organic Food

The participants also emphasized shopping for organic produce at the organic markets and supermarkets. Although domestic consumption of organic food is increasing in Turkey, particularly due to aspirations to lead a healthy life and anxiety about the health of children, it is still limited to environmentally conscious, middle- to high-income consumers (Akgüngör, Miran, and Abay). Selda mentioned that she had tried to buy everything organic until her son was three years old for his health. She emphasized that while she was raising her son organic, she did not even give him vitamins, which is reminiscent of North American mothers' sustainable consumption practices as the gold standard of good mothering (Cairns et al.). Dilek mentioned that she used to shop in the organic pazar every week before moving to her new neighbourhood because, according to her, "everything in the organic market looks fresher and is tastier." Several women mentioned shopping for organic products once in a while, such as pulses, spinach, and chicken. Yet they also shared that they cannot shop for organic products often because of the cost premiums associated with certified organic food.

The participants' remarks about the cost of organic food support previous studies in Turkey, as even the high- to middle-income consumers in Turkey are sensitive to the high cost of organic food. Emine mentioned that she buys tomatoes from the supermarket for one fifth of the price it costs at the organic pazar: "I need to feed a family of five. One kilogram of tomatoes will not be enough for us. Maybe a small family can shop at organic farmers markets. I visited the pazar a couple of times when I was in that neighbourhood. I need to think about my budget." Nevra mentioned shopping for organic products when she was following a specific diet: "The diet was really beneficial to keep my blood level counts normal. But my son, who helped me shop for the organic items, told me that my specific diet was for rich people. I stopped shopping for products after I ran out of my kitchen budget." In contrast, Nevra, a housewife, continued to talk about the benefits of eating only organic products. She also shared that her diet budget was separate from her kitchen budget and that it was "a treat for herself": "My kids are all married, and I have only my retired husband and myself to cook for in the house. My kids and their families come and visit us during the week after their work or over the weekends, and I cook for them. However, my husband was never tight on my kitchen or diet budget." Emine's and Nevra's remarks show that they desire to eat organic food, but their food choices are constrained by their kitchen budget, like consumers elsewhere.

Other challenges related to organic products include the accessibility of organic markets themselves (e.g., they are permanently stationed in one place and open only one day a week). Participants also raised worries about the regulation and enforcement of organic standards and organic pazars. Meryem mentioned the need for independent organic certification: "I spend a lot of money on organic food. I trust only the organic brands of Gökçeada," which is an island in the Aegean Sea. Meryem's remarks are important, as they raise questions about the difficulty of achieving organic production standards in close proximity to urban areas under constant pressure of pollution. Participants also raised questions about natural versus certified organic products. Yasemin said the following:

> After following Mrs. I's farm online sales for four years—you know it is a very well-known natural food place—I have my doubts about what natural food is. She never claimed to have organic certification. I used to buy from her because I believed she was following organic principles. I shopped for her products regularly. Her vegetables used to taste amazing four years ago. I heard from my friends that she has expanded her farm and she purchased from other producers in her village to provide for the expanding number of customers. Do all those farmers follow organic production principles? I am not sure.

Yasemin's concerns about the economies of scale and the expansion of organic production are similar to the discussions about the corporatization of organic agriculture in the United States (Guthman, "Agrarian Dreams"). Even in a country where the majority of organic producers are still small and medium scale, fears and concerns about the co-optation of organic markets show how these markets still function in a similar fashion as conventional agriculture (Le Velly and Dufeu).

Other concerns raised by the participants were about the intersection of organic and halal products. Melda mentioned that she trusts and consumes organic food. However, she added, "I am not sure whether [organic certification agencies] follow all of our halal sensitivities." She mentioned that she purchases poultry that is halal and organic certified. Melda's shopping choices in her quest for clean and healthy food raises new questions about the challenges and possibilities of integrating the demands of the Muslim consumers into the regulation and certification of organic food.

Halal Food

Participants who chose halal products consumed an array of them, from apple juice to biscuits, but they had concerns. Aysin said that "Companies use gelatin in clear fruit juices, but they don't have to label it on the juice package. I need to know that the gelatin comes from halal beef." While religious values were an important factor in choosing halal certified products, the taste was also important. Ceren shared that she likes shopping at the halal market: "I tried many halal products. I like the taste of halal products because they remind me how food used to taste like in my childhood." Although some participants stated that they do not pay much attention to halal certification when they are not travelling abroad, many also acknowledged concerns about the halal status of food production in a Muslim majority country due to agrifood system changes. "I trust halal food brands because I believe they are healthy and good" said Aysin, for example. Almost all participants in Konya and one-fifth of the participants in Ankara said they preferred to shop for halal meat. Although the adulteration with pork (Turkey raises mainly for export markets) was a concern for the participants, the diets of the animals also raised questions of cleanliness. Sibel was suspicious about the sale of wild boar meat mixed with beef meat in hotels and restaurants in tourist resorts in Turkey: "We didn't consume any meat during our vacation last summer."

Concerns about consumption of meat were not limited to beef or pork. Esra said she started consuming free-range chicken and halal chicken because she was concerned about GM animal feed. However, she added, she later stopped cooking chicken in her household: "My hodja[10] said that any chicken can be haram[11] if it does not stay indoors ten days before slaughter. It is the same if they are raised in the villages and can eat the manure of other animals or eat genetically engineered animal feed in big facilities." Although Esra did not specify how her religious leader knew about the halal status of GM feed, her decision to stop eating chicken was partially related to the secondary effects of consuming GM crops.

Yet some participants were also concerned that halal certified food may not address all the values they want in healthy and clean food. Peri mentioned she prefers to shop for halal food, but it is difficult to know whether GM food is halal or not: "I do not buy corn in a cup that is sold in malls because I heard on television that it is not healthy. I know corn has GM ingredients. But I did not hear anything about its halal status." A few of the participants assumed that if it were halal, it would not have GM ingredients. Hatice mentioned that she used to consume Company T's products "because it has halal certification." But then she read in the newspaper that they found GM ingredients in its products. Now, she would not consume that company's products even if they were halal certified. Another focus group discussed the same company. Semiha said she visited Company T's meat slaughterhouse: "It was very hygienic and they follow halal slaughtering practices. Even if they were accused of using GM ingredients, I would trust them." For some participants, the ingredients and their qualities were as important as the halal status, as said by Rusen, "Sometimes it is difficult to match the two [halal and natural]." Tuana mentioned that she follows halal principles in her diet and shops for organic food and added the following: "If I cannot get something directly from the farmer or a vendor I know, I will buy organic items. It is not just about halal. The ingredients of the food, what the processor did, and how it is raised are important for me." Naile, in contrast, wished "There was a 'healthy' label that would combine halal and organic principles." These concerns about the integration of religious values into organic certification can be defined as the consumer's desire for a broader definition of alternative food. Finding such alliances within the alternative food, rather than compartmentalizing it into different certification niche markets, can also bring about long-lasting and structural changes in the agrifood system.

The fragmentation of halal certification and the cost premiums also troubled the participants who shopped for halal food. Semiha complained and asked, "Do halal markets really care about halal food? Maybe they create a new market to sell products in a more expensive way." Similar to the other participants who mentioned the high cost of organic food, halal food shoppers also said they purchase halal-certified food randomly because they cannot afford shopping for all items at halal markets. Semiha continued, "I feel like halal certification has become a trendy thing like organic markets. Halal food items can be two or sometimes three times more expensive than conventional food." These participants also recognized their privilege in their ability to purchase these produces. One participant complained about how halal markets exist side by side conventional agriculture without challenging it.

Although there were only a few companies and civil society organizations that provided halal certification, participants who shopped for halal food said they would shop for brands that they know were owned by trustworthy businessmen who had most of their products halal certified. Yet they also had their doubts about whether the markets providing the best choice and instead emphasized the importance of better government regulations and monitoring. One participant, Saziye, spoke about how a famous company failed a GM ingredient test in baby food in 2014. The failure of this company to enforce its own standards and to live up to its promised values caused conflicting reactions among the participants. "I trusted you," said one participant, "with all my heart." She continued: "I fed my baby their food in jars when my daughter started solids. I was devastated when the media announced the findings of Ministry of Food. Whom can I trust?" The consumer boycotts of the company's products following the media reports on its contaminated baby food are an example of the effectiveness of collective action. The conversation about trust in the focus group sums is representative of the challenges and frustrations of consumers in Turkey. Although these Turkish mothers can shop for alternatives to conventional food to fulfill their values and feed their families healthy food, the options available to them still do not seem to address all of their concerns.

Conclusion

Alternative systems in food provision exist along a spectrum in terms of how they engage with the existing food regime, what they challenge, and what they promise to achieve in terms of access to clean and healthy food (Holt-Gimenez). The quality, safety, and health benefits of food are defined by assembling particular set of conceptions about the food's natural state. Although consumers can trust and know where their food comes from through local food, for consumers with multiple sensitivities, local and organic food may still fall short in addressing their religious concerns. The findings from the focus groups suggest that consumers have multiple concerns in line with their complex identities and values, which are also embedded in their family food work and are constrained by time and/or budget. Yet the compartmentalization of alternative food movement, food certification as well as the social fissures within Turkish society and politics, can prevent unified activism. In general, women were willing to learn about halal food and organic food, but they still were concerned about the lack of regulation in both markets in Turkey and sought further regulation and enforcement by the state.

The unequal division of labour in the household and the gendered nature of food work make women responsible for planning, preparing, and serving healthy meals for their families in the Global North and South. Although women individually choose to shop for clean and healthy food to feed their families, the way in which they share their experiences with other women face to face or through social media reflects the collective impact of their actions. The women in the focus groups complained about food scandals and warnings in the media related to chicken, canola oil, and corn, yet they also talked about the difficulty of choosing healthier or religiously sanctioned food ingredients within the bounds of their budgets. As the investment of time in preparing healthy meals from scratch has become a means to demonstrate appropriate mothering, the participants also emphasized how they take care of their family by making yoghurt at home which is the quintessential test for being a good mother.

The findings show that miscommunication and scientific uncertainty about GM food as well as commercially motivated nutrition advice proffered through media outlets or by celebrity figures contribute to mothers' anxiety about food. The accounts of these mothers reveal that they are conscious of what they should be doing but due to constraints, they do not. These conflicts and ambivalences are also embedded in the routines of mothers' everyday lives. Several participants expressed their concerns about maternal stress and the dilemma of being a good mother while balancing outside-the-home employment with caring for their families. Some women also emphasized that it was burdensome caring for their families by preparing fresh, traditional, and safe foods. However, they were also aware of their privilege in shopping for alternative food and the cost premiums attached to it. Several participants complained about access to organic food and halal food and how access to alternative food creates economic burdens.

The mothers' engagement with alternative food markets and their quest for clean and healthy food in a broader definition has not eliminated their demands for state regulation for food safety. Several women emphasized their lack of trust in both the state and markets, including a lack of trust in schools and other institutions that serve food to their children. Yet even under structural constraints, such as the limited labelling of GM food, mothers as consumers in Turkey have engaged in learning about and avoiding GM food. Although these individual actions seem dispersed and disconnected, women's broader conversations about consumer boycotts of companies using GM ingredients as well as the constraints they face while feeding their families help establish a broader awareness and collective action.

Appendix

Table 1: Educational attainment of focus group participants (n=56)

	Research participants (per cent)	Women in Turkey (per cent)
Illiterate or literate with little or no schooling	0	20
Primary school	7 (n=4)	48
Secondary or primary and secondary	3.5 (n=2)	22
High school	28.5 (n=16)	
Higher education or above	61 (n=34)	10

The data about the educational attainment of women are based on 2013 data from the Turkish Statistics Institute.

Table 2: Economic status of focus group participants (n=56)

Monthly income (Turkish lira)	Monthly income (USD)*	Research participants Per cent
1,000–2,500	418–950	35.7 (n=20)
2,501–4,000	950.1–1,520	21.4 (n=12)
4,000+	1,520.1 +	42.8 (n=24)

*The USD income was calculated based on the Turkish National Bank currency exchange rates of July 15, 2015. The minimum wage at the time of calculations was 1,000 Turkish liras per month (418 USD).

Endnotes

1. Here, I use "Islamic organization" to define an organization that centres the Quran and the Sunnah at the centre of its activities to define food security and what is permissible. Although it is common to define such organizations also as Muslim, in a Muslim-majority country like Turkey, the adjective would not distinguish the framework and focus of such an organization from other organizations that define themselves as secular. Whereas such scholars as Marwan Haddad discuss food security from an Islamic perspective that can be helpful to understand the tenets of an Islamic food security organization, other scholars, such as Huma Ahmed-Ghosh discuss the complexity of demarcating Islamic versus secular movements in Islamic and secular states.

2. The Internet access rate in urban Turkey is over 60 per cent and it keeps increasing. Yet there are differences in terms of Internet access among age groups and by gender. The sixteen to twenty-four age group has the highest rate of internet use. In sixteen and seventy four age group, while 70 per cent of males have internet access only 51 per cent of females have internet access (TUIK).

3. The World Bank defines middle income countries as having a per capita gross national income of US$3,996 to $12,375 based on 2018 data (World Bank).

4. In relation to rising criticisms of the alternative food movement, its composition, goals and effectiveness, there is growing food justice activist community incorporating scholars, activists, food workers, farm workers, people of colour, and women, all in leadership roles as well (Alkon and Guthman).

5. Whereas some participants wore headscarves to represent their religious identity, there were also religiously devout participants without headscarves and secular participants with traditional headscarves. Therefore, participants' religious values—particularly in relation to shopping for halal products or trusting the state authority and the Turkish Directorate for Religious Affairs in terms of regulating food-related issues—only became clarified during the focus groups.

6. About 80 to 85 per cent of Turkey's organically produced fruit, vegetables, and livestock is exported to international markets and the rest is consumed nationally (Ayla).

7. A pseudonym. All names of the research participants have been altered to protect their identity. All English translations of the accounts of the research participants are provided by the author.

8. The National Academy of Sciences in the United States did several reviews of agricultural biotechnology, the most recent of which was in 2016. The reviews focused almost entirely on the genetic aspects of agricultural biotechnology, and after examining epidemiological datasets in the absence of long-term case-controlled studies, they concluded that GM crops pose no unique hazards to human health (National Academies of Science) However, two recent decisions of the World Health Organization's International Agency for Research on Cancer—the classification of glyphosate, the herbicide most widely used on GM crops, as a probable human carcinogen and the herbicide 2,4-dichlorophenoxyacetic acid as a possible human carcinogen—can influence regulators, the public, and policymakers to perform more stringent testing and regulating of GMOs ("Herbicide").

9. There are several natural food and healthy nutrition groups or networks established locally in Ankara, Balikesir, Eskisehir, Canakkale, and Istanbul that can be accessed online. These networks connect producers and consumers through direct marketing, provide

an opportunity for community-supported agriculture for producers, and enable consumers to learn about the production practices of fruit and vegetable producers, mainly in the west and south of the country. The producers in these networks may not have organic certification, but they promise to follow the principles of natural farming established by the networks (see ankaradbb.wordpress.com/katilimci-onay-nedir/).

10. "Hodja" refers to a religious leader.

11. "Haram" can be defined as something not allowed according to Islamic principles.

Works Cited

Adaman, Fikret, Baris Karapinar, and Gokhan Ozertan. *Rethinking Structural Reform in Turkish Agriculture: Beyond the World Bank's Strategy.* Nova Science Publishers, 2010.

Afflerback, Sara, et al. "Infant-Feeding Consumerism in the Age of Intensive Mothering and Risk Society." *Journal of Consumer Culture,* vol. 13 no. 3, 2013, pp. 387-405.

Ahmed-Ghosh, Huma. "Dilemmas of Islamic and Secular Feminists and Feminisms." *Journal of International Women's Studies* vol. 9, no.3, 2008, pp. 99-116.

Akgüngör, Sedef, Bülent Miran, and Canan Abay. "Consumer Willingness to Pay for Organic Food in Urban Turkey." *Journal of International Food & Agribusiness Marketing* vol. 22, no. 3-4, 2010, pp. 299-313.

Alkon, Alison Hope, and Julian Agyeman. *Cultivating Food Justice: Race, Class, and Sustainability.* MIT Press, 2011.

Alkon, Alison Hope, and Julie Guthman. "Introduction." *The New Food Activism: Opposition, Cooperation, and Collective Action,* edited by Alison Hope Alkon and Julie Guthman, 2017, University of California Press, pp. 1-27.

Anderson, Molly. *Charting Growth: Food System Sustainability (Developing Indicators and Measures of Good Food).* Wallace Center at Winrock International, 2009.

Anving, Terese, and Ann-Mari Sellerberg. "Family Meals and Parents' Challenges." *Food, Culture & Society,* vol. 13, no. 2, 2010, pp. 201-14.

Atalan-Helicke, Nurcan, and Becky Mansfield. "Seed Governance at the Intersection of Multiple Global and Nation-State Priorities: Modernizing Seeds in Turkey." *Global Environmental Politics*, vol. 1, no. 4, 2012, pp. 125-46.

Atalan-Helicke, Nurcan. "The Halal Paradox: Negotiating Identity, Religious Values, and Genetically Engineered Food in Turkey." *Agriculture and Human Values*, vol. 32, no. 4, 2015, pp. 663-74.

Atasoy, Yildiz. "Supermarket Expansion in Turkey: Shifting Relations of Food Provisioning." *Journal of Agrarian Change*, vol. 13, no. 4, 2013, pp. 547-70.

Avakian, Arlene Voski, and Barbara Haber. *From Betty Crocker to Feminist Food Studies: Critical Perspectives on Women and Food.* Liverpool University Press, 2005.

Ayla, Dilara. *Türkiye'de Organik Tarım (Organic Agriculture in Turkey).* 2002. Trabzon: Karadeniz Teknik Üniversitesi Sosyal Bilimler Enstitüsü, PhD dissertation.

"Bakan Çelik'ten GDO denetimi açıklaması." ("Minister Celik's Statement on GMO Food Monitoring.") *Milliyet*, 21 Mar. 2017, www.milliyet.com.tr/ekonomi/son-dakika-bakan-celikten-gdo-denetimi-aciklamasi-2417735. Accessed 1 June 2020.

Beck, Ulrich. *Risk Society: Towards a New Modernity.* Sage, 1992.

Bellows, Anne C., Gabriela Alcaraz, and William K. Hallman. "Gender and Food, a Study of Attitudes in the USA Towards Organic, Local, US Grown, and GM-Free Foods." *Appetite*, vol. 55, no. 3, 2010, pp. 540-50.

Cairns, Kate, et al. "The Caring, Committed Eco-Mom: Consumption Ideals and Lived Realities of Toronto Mothers." *Green Consumption: The Global Rise of Eco-Chic*, edited by Bart Barendregt and Ricke Jaffe, R., 2014, Bloomsbury Publishing. pp. 100-14.

Cairns, Kate, and Josée Johnston. *Food and Femininity.* Bloomsbury Publishing, 2015.

Counihan, Carole. *Around the Tuscan Table: Food, Family, and Gender in Twentieth-Century Florence.* Routledge, 2004.

DBB. "Natural Food, Conscious Nutrition. Community Contract." *DBB*, 2019. dogalbilinclibeslenme.wordpress.com/topluluk-sozlesmesi/. Accessed 1 June 2020.

Delen, Nafiz, et al. "Türkiye'de Pestisit Kullanimi, Kalıntı ve Orga-nizmalarda Duyarlılık Azalışı Sorunları." ("Pesticide Use in Tur-key, Residue Issues and Sensitivity Declines."). *Türkiye Ziraat Müh-endisligi,* vol. 6, 2005, pp. 3-7.

Désilets, Marie-Claude, et al. "Dietary Transition Stages Based on Eat-ing Patterns and Diet Quality among Haitians of Montreal, Cana-da." *Public Health Nutrition,* vol. 10, no. 5, 200, pp. 454-63.

DeVault, Marjorie L. *Feeding the Family: The Social Organization of Caring as Gendered Work.* University of Chicago Press, 1994.

DuPuis, E. Melanie, Jill Lindsey Harrison, and David Goodman. "Just Food." *Cultivating Food Justice: Race, Class, and Sustainability,* edited by Alison Hope Alkon and Julian Agyeman, 2011, pp. 263-82.

Eryılmaz, G. A., Demiryürek, K., and Emir, M. "Avrupa Birliği ve Türkiye'de organik tarım ve gıda ürünlerine karşı tüketici davranışları." ("Organic Agriculture in Turkey and the European Union and Consumer Behaviour.") *Anadolu Tarım Bilimleri Dergisi,* vol. 30, no. 2, 2015, pp. 199-206.

Fischer, Johan. *The Halal Frontier.* Springer, 2011.

Fuentes, Maria, and Christian Fuentes. "Risk Stories in the Media: Food Consumption, Risk and Anxiety." *Food, Culture & Society,* vol. 18, no. 1, 2015, pp. 71-87.

GIMDES. "Hazir Lokma Artinca, Helal Lokma Unutulunca, Anneli-gin Onemi Yitirilince." ("When Processed Food Increases, Halal Food Is Forgotten, and the Value of Motherhood Is Lost.") *GIMDES Dergi,* no. 21, 2011, pp. 8-9.

"Herbicide 2, 4-D 'Possibly' Causes Cancer, World Health Organ-isation Study Finds." *The Guardian,* 15 June 2015, www.theguardian.com/environment/2015/jun/23/herbicide-24-d-possibly-causes-cancer-world-health-organisation-study-finds Accessed 1 June 2020.

Guthman, Julie. "Neoliberalism and the Making of Food Politics in California." *Geoforum,* vol. 39, 2008, pp. 1171-83.

Guthman, Julie. "Fast Food/Organic Food: Reflexive Tastes and the Making of 'Yuppie Chow.'" *Social & Cultural Geography,* vol. 4, no.1, 2003, pp. 45-58.

Guthman, Julie. Agrarian Dreams: The Paradox of organic farming in California. University of California Press, 2004.

Haddad, Marwan. "An Islamic Perspective on Food Security Management." *Water Policy*, vol. 14, no. S1, 2012, pp. 121-35.

Hays, Sharon. *The Cultural Contradictions of Motherhood*. Yale University Press, 1998.

Holt-Giménez, Eric. "Food Security, Food Justice, or Food Sovereignty." *Cultivating Food Justice: Race, Class, and Sustainability*, edited by Alison Hope Alkon and Julian Agyeman, MIT Press, 2011, pp. 309-30.

Jackson, Peter. *Anxious Appetites: Food and Consumer Culture*. Bloomsbury Publishing, 2015.

Jaffee, Daniel. *Brewing Justice: Fair Trade Coffee, Sustainability, and Survival*. University of California Press, 2014.

Johnston, Josée, and Michelle Szabo. "Reflexivity and the Whole Foods Market Consumer: The Lived Experience of Shopping for Change." *Agriculture and Human Values* vol. 28, no. 3, 2011, pp. 303-19.

Kadak, Şelale. "Mamalar GDOlu mu değil mi." ("Which Baby Food Has GMOs.") *Sabah Daily* 2010, www.sabah.com.tr/yazarlar/kadak/2010/02/03/mamalar_gdolu_mu_degil_mi_hangi_mamalar_gdolu_boyle_onemli_bir_konu_nasil_gundem_disi_kaldi. Accessed 1 June 2020.

Kenanoğlu Bektaş, Zerrin and Özlem Karahan Uysal, "Türkiye'de Geleneksel ve Organik Ürün Fiyatları Üzerine Bir Değerlendirme." ("An Evaluation of the Conventional and Organic Product Prices in Turkey.") Tenth National Agricultural Economy Congress Proceedings, 5-7 Sept. 2012, www.tarimarsiv.com/wp-content/uploads/2017/05/350-360.pdf. Accessed 1 June 2020.

Kinchy, Abby. *Seeds, Science, and Struggle: The Global Politics of Transgenic Crops*. MIT Press, 2012.

Le Velly, Ronan, and Ivan Dufeu. "Alternative Food Networks as 'Market Agencements': Exploring Their Multiple Hybridities." *Journal of Rural Studies* vol. 43, 2016, pp. 173-82.

Mansfield, Becky. "Environmental Health as Biosecurity: 'Seafood Choices,' Risk, and the Pregnant Woman as Threshold." *Annals of the Association of American Geographers*, vol. 102, no. 5, 2012, pp. 969-76.

Marshall, D. "Images of Motherhood: Food Advertising in Good Housekeeping Magazine 1950–2010." *Motherhoods, Markets and*

Consumption: The Making of Mothers in Contemporary Western Cultures, edited by Stephanie O'Donohoe et al., Routledge, 2014, pp. 116-27.

McNaughton, Darlene. "From the Womb to the Tomb: Obesity and Maternal Responsibility." Critical Public Health, vol. 21, no. 2, 2011, pp. 179-90.

Mumyakmaz, Alper. "Elitlerin Yeni Yüzü, Islami Burjuvazi." ("The New Face of Elites, Islamic Borgeoisie.") Mustafa Kemal Üniversitesi Sosyal Bilimler Enstitüsü Dergisi, vol. 11, no. 27, 2014, pp. 367-382.

National Academies of Science. "Genetically Engineered Crops: Experiences and Prospects." NAP, Report in Brief 2016, www.nap.edu/resource/23395/GE-crops-report-brief.pdf. Accessed 1 June 2020.

OECD Trade and Agriculture Directorate. Agricultural Policy Monitoring and Evaluation: OECD Countries and Emerging Economies. OECD Publishing, 2011.

Oğuz, Özdemir. "Attitudes of Consumers toward the Effects of Genetically Modified Organisms (GMOs): The Example of Turkey." Journal of Food, Agriculture & Environment, vol. 7, no. 3 and 4, 2009, pp. 159-65.

Öztürk, Sibel, Safiye Ağapınar Şahin, and Fatma Guducu Tüfekçi. "Annelerin Genetiği Değiştirilmiş Organizmalara Yönelik Bilgi Durumları Ve Tutumları." İzmir Dr.Behçet Uz Çocuk Hastanesi Dergisi, vol. 4, no. 2, 2014, pp. 117-22.

Pasche Guignard, Floreance. "Nurturing the Sustainable Family: Natural Parenting and Environmentalist Foodways in Francophone Contexts." Mothers and Food: Negotiating Foodways from Maternal Perspectives, edited by Florence Pasche Guignard and Tanya M. Cassidy, Demeter Press, 2016, pp. 55-69.

Parsons, Julie M. "When Convenience Is Inconvenient: 'Healthy' Family Foodways and the Persistent Intersectionalities of Gender and Class." Journal of Gender Studies. vol. 25, no. 4, 2016, pp. 382-97.

Pingali, Prabhu. "Agricultural Policy and Nutrition Outcomes—Getting beyond the Preoccupation with Staple Grains." Food Security, vol. 7, no. 3, 2015, pp. 583-91.

Popkin, Barry M., Linda S. Adair, and Shu Wen Ng. "Global Nutrition Transition and the Pandemic of Obesity in Developing Countries." Nutrition Reviews, 2012, vol. 70, no. 1, pp. 3-21.

Roff, Robin Jane. "Shopping for Change? Neoliberalizing Activism and the Limits to Eating Non-GMO." *Agriculture and Human Values*, vol. 24, no. 4, 2007, pp. 511-22.

Sağlık Bakanlığı. "Türkiye Beslenme Rehberi." ("Turkey Nutrition Guide.") *Republic of Turkey Ministry of Health*, Report 1031, 2016, hsgm.saglik.gov.tr/depo/birimler/saglikli-beslenme-hareketli-hayat-db/Yayinlar/kitaplar/Kitaplar-eski/Turkiye-Beslenme-Rehberi-Turkce.pdf. Accessed 1 June 2020.

Sarıkaya, Nilgün. "Organik ürün tüketimini etkileyen faktörler ve tutumlar üzerine bir saha çalışması." ("Factors Affecting Organic Food Consumption and a Field Study") *Kocaeli Üniversitesi Sosyal Bilimler Enstitüsü Dergisi*, vol. 14, no. 2, 2007, pp. 110-25.

Sert, Esra. "GDO'suz ürün isteyen anne bin kaplan gücünde." ("Mothers Demanding Non-GMO Food Are as Strong as a Thousand Tigers."), www.ntv.com.tr/turkiye/gdosuz-urun-isteyen-anne-bin-kaplan-gucunde,6WUI-QIKV0WPYQQ-J2ku-g. Accessed 1 June 2020.

Sodjinou, Roger, V. Agueg, B. Fayomi and H. Delisle. "Dietary Patterns of Urban Adults in Benin: Relationship with Overall Diet Quality and Socio-Demographic Characteristics." *European Journal of Clinical Nutrition*, vol. 63 no. 2, 2009, pp. 222-228.

Stolle, Dietlind and Michele Micheletti. *Political Consumerism: Global Responsibility in Action.* Cambridge University Press, 2013.

Tarım Orman. "Organik Tarım İstatistikleri." ("Organic Agriculture Statistics.") *Ministry of Agriculture and Forestry*, www.tarimorman.gov.tr/Konular/Bitkisel-Uretim/Organik-Tarim/Istatistikler. Accessed 1 June 2020.

Tuğal, Cihan. "Fight Or Acquiesce? Religion and Political Process in Turkey's and Egypt's Neoliberalizations." *Development and Change*, vol. 43, no. 1, 2012, pp. 23-51.

Tuik."Hanehalkı Bilişim Teknolojileri Kullanım Araştırması 2016." ("Household Surveys of Access to Computer and Internet Technologies.") *Tuik*, tuik.gov.tr/PreHaberBultenleri.do?id=21779. Accessed 1 June 2020.

Tüsev. "Yemezler Kampanyası Vaka Analizi." ("Case Study of We Won't Eat Campaign.") *Report of Third Sector Foundation of Turkey,*

2013, www.tusev.org.tr/usrfiles/images/YemezlerVakaAnalizi TR.06.11.13.pdf. Accessed 1 June 2020.

"Ünlü bebek mamasında GDO çıktı." ("Famous Babyfood Has GMOs.") *Sabah*, 2014, www.sabah.com.tr/aktuel/2014/05/26/ unlu-bebek-mamasinda-gdo-cikti. Accessed 1 June 2020.

Willis, Margaret M., and Juliet B. Schor. "Does Changing a Light Bulb Lead to Changing the World? Political Action and the Conscious Consumer." *The ANNALS of the American Academy of Political and Social Science*, vol. 644, no.1, 2012, pp. 160-190.

World Bank "World Bank country and lending groups" https:// datahelpdesk.worldbank.org/knowledgebase/articles/906519- world-bank-country-and-lending-groups. Accessed 10 June 2020.

ZMO. "Çiftçi sayısı arttı, üretim düştü." ("The Number of Organic Farmers Has Increased, Total Production Has Decreased."), *Turkish Chamber of Agricultural Engineeres*, 23 July 2019, zmo.org.tr/genel/ bizden_detay.php?kod=31620&tipi=24&sube=0. Accessed 1 June 2020.

Death to Us and Ghost Nets

Dara Herman Zierlein

Part III

Expressions of Apocalyptic Themes

We Won't Be Fertile

Dara Herman Zierlein

Ophelia's Drowning

Dara Herman Zierlein

Chapter Five

The Maternalocene: The (In)Fertility of Mother Nature in Postapocalyptic Narrative

Dwayne Avery

Storytelling in the Anthropocene: Mothers in a Time of Planetary Crisis

In *Staying with Trouble: Making Kin in the Chthulucene*, Donna Haraway describes environmental storytelling as a risky business that is doubly troubling: not only is it essential that we create inclusive stories, but it matters which stories we use to tell other stories with. As Haraway writes: "It matters what matters we use to think other matters with ... it matters what knots knot knots, what thoughts think thoughts, what descriptions describe descriptions, what ties tie ties. It matters what stories make worlds, what worlds make stories" (12). In this chapter, I explore some of the family dramas postapocalyptic cinema uses to tell the story of environmental disaster and the role mothers play in the Anthropocene.[1] Dismissed by some as a dying art incapable of holding our attention, cinema today has returned with an ecological vengeance. Cinema may even be the paradigmatic art of the Anthropocene, "an allegory for the fiery ends of the world" (Wark, "Anthropo{mise-en-s}cène"). Indeed, by portraying the anxiety, loss, and precarity bound up with the prospect of planetary extinction, it is no wonder that postapocalyptic cinema has become the go-to genre for registering the violent asymmetries of life in the Anthropocene.

However, while many look to postapocalyptic culture for clues to living well in an age of planetary uncertainty, few acknowledge the genre's explication of the domestic fissures and parental rearrangements produced by the threat of environmental catastrophe. This is an unfortunate omission since by focusing on "humanity's" new geologic agency, dominant Anthropocene stories fail to recognize how fear is worked out primarily through the architecture of ordinary life. The dangers of climate heating, rising sea levels, food shortages, and war are not threats that lurk out there in some undefined location. Nor are they, despite the current tendency to conflate the Anthropocene with the perilous advancement of "Human Civilization," felt by an unmarked human condition. Instead, catastrophes are immanent accidents deeply intertwined with specific homes and family arrangements. As Franklin and Cromby write, "It is the family unit where this culture of fear is perhaps most visible as the relationship between adults and children is seemingly more fraught than ever" (161).

What I wish to argue here is that the fear of planetary collapse offers opportunities for reassessing contemporary attitudes about parenting. Like the horror film, which reveals "the contemporary weakening of patriarchal authority and the glaring contradictions that exist between the mythology of family relations and their actual social practices" (Sobchack 147), postapocalyptic narratives expose society's embedded norms about mothering and offer a "call to engage in resistant readings of hegemonic" family structures (Bressler and Lengel 38). As caretakers, whose lives involve protecting children from countless daily hazards, mothers stand at the forefront of the risk society. However, until now, there has been little research exploring how the maternal overtones of the family drama converge with environmental disaster films. Not only do postapocalyptic narratives set the stage for the creation of new family arrangements, such as communal parenting, but in their attention to matters of care they provide clues to the origins of the Anthropocene and offer ongoing resources for living amid the ruins of ecological crisis. I call this maternal understanding of the Anthropocene "the Maternalocene."

Like other ecofeminists, my maternalistic understanding of postapocalyptic culture foregrounds how thinking with the Anthropocene requires paying attention to maternal labour and care—both the violent and hopeful ways bodily matter meshes with other kinds of earthbound matter. In doing so, I hope to show that the Anthropocene is as much about populating the earth with new stories about inhabiting the planet as it is about marking the beginnings of a new epochal shift in geologic time (Bonneuil and Fressoz). As Haraway argues, the story of the Anthropocene is troubling not because it insists on the planetary burdens we now face; there is no doubting the precarity of contemporary life. Rather, the trouble with most Anthropocene stories is that they cast a set of totalizing universal actors (Humankind, Man the Tool Maker...), that insist on the inevitability of failure. Claiming "the game is over" (Lovelock) or "we are already dead" (Brassier) not only entraps us in isolating despair but denies our ability to work and play for a resurgent world (Haraway, *Staying with Trouble* 3). "We need another figure," Haraway writes, "a thousand names of something else, to erupt out of the Anthropocene into another big-enough story" (*Staying with Trouble* 52).

Haraway's answer to paternalistic readings of the Anthropocene is to recast it as the Chthulucene, a metaphoric figure comprised of a host of tentacle-like creatures that show natureculture's intricate web of symbiotic relationships. For Haraway, these other images of Gaia transform the Anthropocene's drama of planetary extinction into situated practices involving multiple other places and a myriad of other nonhuman creatures. They also point to a different understanding of precarious time. Whereas the Anthropocene's dominant story marks the current age as an emergency, a crisis-prone temporality of unrelenting threat and fear, the Chthulucene is a time of urgent ongoingness—a time of collective labour where we continue making new material kinships with others.

Building on Haraway's notion that making trouble means making kin, I offer a maternalistic understanding of the Anthropocene. At first glance, this move may seem troubling for a different set of reasons. Historically, using images or metaphors of motherhood to describe nature has been a contested and divisive practice within many strands of ecofeminism. In her overview of feminist debates about the mother-nature dyad, Catherine Roach describes three conflicting schools of thought, which respond to the questions: Are women closer to nature, and is nature a kind of mother? Those that answer "yes" often endorse some kind of essentialism (biological essentialism, strategic essentialism), which links environmental destruction and gender inequalities to fight patriarchy. Those that answer "no" often rely on social constructionist critiques, which deny essentialisms of any sort. This move usually rejects the mother-nature dyad entirely and places women within the spheres of human culture, subjectivity, and sovereignty. For Roach, neither approach is satisfactory. Endorsing a third school of thought, she claims that to affirm or deny the mother-nature dyad on these terms is untenable since they rely upon a dualistic understanding of nature and society. For Roach, envisioning life as a web of interconnections requires a new political ecology that "shifts the viewpoint of the first two and seeks to melt down their rigidity by making their concepts of 'nature' and 'culture' less rigid or fixed and more 'biodegradable' or environmentally sound" (54).

Given the problematic place of motherhood in environmental thinking, why use a matricentric framework to engage in a feminist politics for the Anthropocene? Here, I outline three reasons why framing the Anthropocene in terms of maternal thinking is not only fruitful but necessary. First, at the precise moment when feminist debates about Mother Nature appear exhausted, the Anthropocene brings a renewed interest in gendering nature. Although some worry about the Anthropocene's reclamation of "Man's" exceptionality, equally worrisome is how some use contradictory maternal metaphors to understand the return of nature. Both a stern and vindictive maternal force that keeps us in line and a weak and exhausted resource in need of our protection, nature in the Anthropocene is as much about the return of regressive gender politics as it is about the reestablishment of humanistic theories of Man. In French-language theories of the Anthropocene alone, one encounters a plethora of stories that call upon Mother Earth or Gaia as metaphors for a planetary understanding of human-nature relations. In his canonical work on the politics of the new earth sciences, Bruno Latour deliberately uses Lovelock's Gaia hypothesis (a theory already critiqued by feminists) to draw attention to our earthbound place in the world (*Facing Gaia*). The feminist philosopher of science, Isabelle Stengers, also calls upon Gaia to understand capitalism's relationship to environmental catastrophe. For Stengers, if nature is a mother, she is an irritable caretaker that should not be offended. Perhaps the most enthusiastic French thinker to use Mother Earth metaphors is Michel Serres. In his book, *Biogea*, Serres reminds us that nature means to be born. For Serres, nature is not an essence or a limitless resource but a series of births calling our attention to the fertility and vitality of the Great Mother.

Outside this strand of French-language theory, the gendering of nature continues in many overt forms. In 2015, artist Alexandra Pirici and curator Raluca Voinea released their "Manifesto for the Gynecene," a maternalistic tract contending that we must think our new geological era through feminine experiences of care, emancipation, and peace. Whereas such writers as Pirici and Voinea appear to be critically aware of the broader political implications of treating nature as a mother, it is not clear whether others, such as Latour, are well versed in feminist debates that problematize the convergence of women and nature. Given the uncritical employment of these new motherhood metaphors, it becomes necessary to reexamine the mother-nature dyad so that thinking about the Anthropocene does not slip back into misogynistic stereotypes.

Second, popular culture often imagines the global ecological crisis through the inner workings of home. From television shows, films, and advertisements to political campaigns, environmental summits, and green living promotions, popular media posits an isomorphic relationship between ecological health and domestic viability. Sometimes this focus on the health of domestic living challenges our understanding of what is at stake in the growing degradation of the planet. When global concerns about environmental toxicity, the precarity of children's health, and resource depletion form a moral economy of home, we encounter a politicization of the personal that can raise ecological concerns to a geological level. It is this awareness of the precarity of home that lies at the heart of many postapocalyptic narratives. By showing characters trying to salvage new kinships amid the ruins of catastrophe, postapocalyptic cinema is a genre that at once shows us the uncertainty of the future and the constant need to forge new family relationships in the present.

At the same time, mainstream media continues to trade on idealized images of family life to raise ecological awareness. In its most mystifying form, the valorization of the all-nurturing good mother lends support to a neoliberal framework whereby environmental destruction is condensed to the matter of proper domesticity. Celebrating the self-sacrificing work of the ecofriendly housewife, this brand of green capitalism imagines we can avert ecological collapse through the eternal labour of good housekeeping. Using pristine and pastoral images of the ecofriendly home can also lead to rarified understandings of nature that gloss over the complexity of global environmental issues. Like the "Love Your Mother" slogans from previous activist movements, many populist campaigns sentimentalize the link between child, mother, and nature to produce a romanticized idea of nature entirely at odds with the earth sciences. As Rebekah Sheldon reminds us, this myopic chain of signifiers often provides a static and benign version of nature that robs it of any diversity, instability, and complexity.

Third, despite the many pitfalls of aligning mothers with nature, mothering continues to be an essential activist strategy for politicizing the personal. Grounded in the material realities, labour, and knowledge associated with caring for children, the maternal activist diverges from the environmental idealizations found in popular media. Maternal activism forms a politics from the bottom, which translates the protection of children (Ruddick) into a public resource bringing awareness to the environmental plights of those who may not have a political voice. As Susan Logsdon-Conradsen writes: "Throughout history, mother activists have utilized the symbolic power of the mother archetype to legitimize their activism, garner public support, and motivate others to join their causes. In addition to being used strategically, environmental activists across time describe being inspired by their roles as mothers to become activists" (10). A strength of these maternal activist movements is that they have stuck through many periods of environmental crisis. As such, they come equipped with many strategies for bringing to the fore issues some dismiss as parochial or personal. From local concerns over the toxic effects of industry on children's health and the need to preserve animal habitats to clear air initiatives and worries over global environmental justice, maternal activists' work provides ongoing resources for collective knowledge and action.

To engage these larger debates, my understanding of the Maternalocene borrows from matricentric feminists, who define mothering through two superimposed meanings. The first meaning sees motherhood as a patriarchal institution that uses female reproduction to ensure that, in the words of Adrienne Rich, "all women remain under male control" (13). The second meaning refers to acts of mothering—the situated knowledge, labour, and practices of care stemming from women's experiences with what Sara Ruddick calls "maternal thinking." As Andrea O'Reilly writes, "While motherhood, as an institution, is a male-defined site of oppression, women's own experiences of mothering can nonetheless be a source of power" (3). Exploring both the oppressive and empowering nature of maternity, the Maternalocene shows how thinking about the Anthropocene requires apprehending both crisis and cure; it invites forms of storytelling that allow us to look for life amid the ruins of global precarity. Just as many maternal feminists understand mother-hood as an exploitative system that extracts surplus value by subjugating female labour, the Maternalocene strives to visualize the climate injust-ices and gender disparities bound up with environmental destruction. Staying with the trouble also requires avoiding the rhetoric of emergency that sees failure as the only option. To meet this challenge, I use the Maternalocene to draw upon the practices of care needed to make what Haraway (*Staying with Trouble*) calls oddkin—the unexpected material assemblages that join strangers in complicated and fragile coalitions of care.

Postapocalyptic Cinema: Climate Change, Narrative, and Feminist Politics

According to novelist and critic Amitav Ghosh, the problem of climate change converges with another unprecedented breakdown: the failure of the cultural imaginary to grasp the strange and improbable times we are living. For Ghosh, the challenge of the Anthropocene is as much a literary problem as it is a problem of environmental sustainability. We are living in wild times, Ghosh writes, a period of extraordinary uncer-tainty that writers fail to take seriously. Naming this deficiency in the cultural imagination "the great derangement," Ghosh is adamant we can no longer call upon art and literature to apprehend the urgency of the times. Serious literature (which for Ghosh corresponds to the bourgeois novel) has little to say about climate change, and by filling in ordinary life with petty bourgeois pleasures, creates "a form of serious-ness that is blind to potentially life-changing threats" (16).

Ghosh's problem is that he fails to acknowledge the genre that takes climate change seriously—namely, the strange and improbable worlds of science fiction. Dismissing sci-fi as frivolous escapism, Ghosh writes, "It is as though in the literary imagination climate change were somehow akin to extra-terrestrials or inter-planetary travel" (16). However, it is precisely within the genre of science fiction that the cultural imaginary negotiates the torrential times we live. From environmental disaster films such as *Gravity, Geostorm,* and *The Day After Tomorrow* to extra-terrestrial thrillers such as *District 9, Avatar,* and *Prometheus,* science fiction films offer a surplus of stories about humans manufacturing conditions for their own demise. Thus the challenge today is not so much that the cultural imaginary neglects the alarming possibilities of climate change; instead, the more significant problem is how genres, such as science fiction, often use the risk of calamity to recuperate dangerous ideas about humanity's exceptionality and society's need for new paternalistic protectors.

This trend is most evident in extinction narratives that invite the viewer to appreciate a flourishing world of nonhumans by imagining one where humans are absent or on the verge of extinction. In such films as *After Earth, I Am Legend,* or *The Book of Eli,* the threat of human extinction becomes an opportunity to contemplate how nonhuman agencies (e.g., feral animals, zombies, and nuclear radiation) undermine the prospect of human progress. The 2016 documentary *Homo Sapiens* takes this macabre experiment to the extreme as the camera testifies to humanity's failure to protect the earth by showing a planet devoid of all human presence. Like Alan Weisman's book *The World Without Us, Homo Sapiens* uses the paradoxical thought experiment of visualizing a world without humans to prop up the claim that the human species acts as an unprecedented geological force.

In varying degrees, what the extinction narrative attempts is a cinematic version of what the philosopher Eugene Thacker calls the spectral and speculative "world-without-us" (Thacker 4-8). To meet the challenge of global climate change, Thacker insists that we need to conceptualize the planet without relying upon a worldview that prioritizes humans. The "world-without-us," Thacker asserts, provides this new speculative line of thinking. Unlike the "world-for-us" (the world of human culture and meaning) or the "world-in-itself" (the world of nature we envision through human eyes), the "world-without-us" refers to a speculative perspective that allows us to grasp the nonhuman by subtracting humans from the world. For Thacker, by imagining a planetary system that persists without humans, the "world-without-us" attunes us to non-human agencies and that there are truths out there that exceed human meaning.

Although the aim of the "world-without-us" is to heighten our appreciation of nonhumans, most times, the fantasy of extinction bolsters the exceptionality of strong men. For example, in many "last man standing" films, the collapse of society acts as a pretext for reclaiming the paternalism of heroic fathers, whose extraordinary feats of violence seek to tame nature rather than liberate it from the clutches of human thinking. Even the desire to stand outside the planet's messy interconnections to gain knowledge of a world without humans cannot untangle itself from a long history of abstract, masculinist thinking. Like the famous Blue Marble image of earth, which offered viewers a disembodied view far outside the messy entanglements of life, extinction narratives thrive on a godlike perspective from nowhere, avoiding the complexities of human-nature relations. Who exactly is the "us" in the "world-without-us?" As Rob Nixon shows, the destruction wrought by climate change, toxic pollution, and species extinction is far from even. Most times it is the poor, or what Kevin Bales calls "disposable people," who must bear the burden of what Nixon calls "slow violence": an invisible and insidious form of violence involving disasters that are slow moving, anonymous, and indifferent to the sensationalistic narratives covered by contemporary media.

By indiscriminately imagining a world erased of human agency, extinction narratives conform to the "dominant visual apparatus of the Anthropocene" (Alaimo). As Stacey Alaimo writes:

> And once again, in the dominant visual apparatus of the Anthropocene, the viewer enjoys a comfortable position outside the systems depicted. The already iconic images of the Anthropocene ask nothing from the human spectator; they make no claim; they neither involve nor implore. The images make risk, harm, and suffering undetectable, as toxic and radioactive regions do not appear, nor do the movements of climate refugees. The geographies of the sixth great extinction are not evident. The perspective is predictable and reassuring, despite its claim to novelty and cataclysm. (92)

As Alamio makes clear about the larger story of the Anthropocene, the danger in desiring a "world-without-us" is that too many human things (labour, gender inequalities, the precarity of the poor) end up being eclipsed by the desire to step outside a world of human agency. Thus one of the most pressing challenges emerging from the Anthropocene is that in addition to living in "a new phase of history in which nonhumans are no longer excluded (Morton 2013 12), we must also grapple with a new phase of geology in which humans are included.

Another trend in contemporary film responding to Josh Lepawsky's call to become "more sensitive and responsive to the fragilities" of our life support systems centres on the mother-child dyad. Unlike the extinction narrative's thanatopolitics, which purports to raise ecological awareness by contemplating the ends of man, the mother-child figuration opens a politics of natality, wherein acting together leads to unexpected kinships. Focusing on the situated knowledge, care practices, and maternal labour that foster new forms of life, the mother-child dyad makes explicit what Timothy Morton calls the "symbiotic real"—the way human life depends upon solidarity with human and nonhuman support systems (*Humankind*). In such fantastical films as *Okja* and *Beasts of the Southern Wild,* children emerge as exemplary practitioners of the art of becoming-with nonhumans. Creating strong bonds of solidarity with animals, children in these films intermesh in material and affective relationships unavailable to adults. In other post-apocalyptic disaster films, such as *Snowpiercer* and *The Road,* not only are children subjected to unthinkable horrors, calling attention to the need for maternal care and protection, but they also emerge as reproductive signs of the planet's hopeful future.

The series of films and television shows that interest me envision ecological crisis through women's maternal capacities. From such television shows as *The Lottery* and *The Handmaid's Tale* to such films as *Mad Max: Fury Road* and *Children of Men,* a primary way the media responds to the Anthropocene involves posting an isomorphic relationship between the planet's environmental degradation and women's fertility. It would be easy to dismiss these stories as ecological versions of the good-bad mother dichotomy, wherein mothers carry the burden of blame for global environmental catastrophe. This reactionary response, however, fails to acknowledge how these narratives open a feminist politics for the Anthropocene. In what follows, I bring together the films *Mad Max: Fury Road* and *Children of Men* to show the political importance of thinking about ecological crisis through the Maternalocene. This merger of films, however, should not be underestimated. On their own, neither film can articulate the ongoing struggles, hopes, and maternal becomings bound up with the Anthropocene. Taken together, however, they map the two cornerstones of the Maternalocene. *Fury Road,* for example, shows how we need to think about the Anthropocene via climate justice; how certain bodies and labour practices bear the burden of the fallout of environmental destruction. In *Children of Men*, extinction becomes an opportunity to think about how a maternal politics of care may act as an ongoing resource for forging ahead in new coalitions with others.

Cheap Nature: *Mad Max* and the Politics of Maternal Abjection

Offering a hyperbolic thrill ride through a postapocalyptic wasteland ravaged by war, drought, and famine, one would think *Fury Road* functions as a prime example of Ghosh's great derangement. From start to finish, *Fury Road* is pure spectacle, Hollywood at its most explosive and entertaining. A Monster Jam on steroids, the film seemingly offers viewers little more than a high-octane road movie, where the rumble of engines and the splatter of blood override the genre's concern with collective hubris. When Furiosa (Charlize Theron) helps the Five Wives escape the Citadel, all hell breaks loose, as Immortan Joe (Hugh Keays-Byrne), the Citadel's patriarchal overlord, unleashes his army of War Boys to track down his prized possessions. What ensues is a maddening two-hour chase-scene with Furiosa and Max (Tom Hardy) trying to outrun the War Boys and reach the Green Place, a matriarchal refuge in the desert.

Although the film's incessant pyrotechnics may deter some from viewing it as a climate change narrative, one of *Fury Road's* strengths resides in its explosive spectacle. Through its parodic combustion of fossil fuels (known in the film as "guzzoline"), the film shows one of the primary causes of anthropogenic global warming. This alone is remarkable. Most postapocalyptic films are content to focus on the horrendous results of catastrophe rather than pinpoint the reasons behind the effects. Indeed, what *Fury Road* imagines is not the fallout of a fossil fuel society but its violent continuity: the film's pimped-out cars, its furious and explosive chase scenes, its maniacal displays of gasoline frenzy all point to what McKenzie Wark calls modernity's most significant and detrimental act of liberation: "The Carbon Liberation Front." Wark writes the following:

Of all the liberation movements of the eighteenth, nineteenth and twentieth centuries, one succeeded without limit. It did not liberate a nation, or a class, or a colony, or a gender, or a sexuality. What it freed was not the animals, and still less the cyborgs, although it was far from human. What it freed was a chemical, an element: carbon. A central theme of the Anthropocene was and remains the story of the Carbon Liberation Front ... The Anthropocene is a redistribution, not of wealth, or power, or recognition, but of molecules. (*Molecular Red* 9-10)

Perhaps no other film shows the tremendous fury and devastation associated with The Carbon Liberation Front. Like the Anthropocene, *Fury Road* runs on pure carbon, its ferocious spectacle a testament to the metabolic rifts created by capitalism's desire to unearth energy. The film, however, does not stop at identifying the bio-chemical causes of the Anthropocene; it also illustrates how redistributing fossil fuels depends upon the capitalistic conversion of differences into "differentials" (Clover and Spahr). To generate surplus value, capitalism encloses lived differences, from the ecological differences between oceans, coral reefs, marine wetlands, and forests to differences in domestic labour, within a property rights system that treats everything as a homogenized commodity. As Clover and Spahr write, domestic labour "functions for capital not as difference but as differential, as a socially arbitrated and ideologically naturalized gap ... across which surplus value flows. It is a sort of development of underdevelopment at the level of the household" (153).

Just as feminists have shown that unpaid maternal care is instrumental to the maintenance of a healthy workforce, in *Fury Road* the differential used to redistribute fossil fuels is the abject labour of motherhood: underpinning the steady flow of fossil fuels is the steady flow of mother's milk. We see this abject differential in an opening scene: as Immortan Joe inspects a bottle of breastmilk, a group of lactating mothers sit in the background, their labouring bodies hooked up to an elaborate milking machine. The mothers, we learn later, constitute an invaluable resource for the Citadel, providing an elite drink used to trade for guzzoline. Besides delivering a constant flow of breastmilk, the Citadel's women also perform a biopolitical function. Like the lactating mothers, the Five Wives are a select group of women, whose bodies act as breeding machines for the Citadel's patriarchal elite. Locked inside a vault, the Wives possess little value outside their status as reproductive property.

In the birthing scene, their designation as abject matter becomes insidiously clear: when one of the pregnant wives suffers severe injuries from a car crash, Immortan Joe demands that her body be savagely cut open to save the unborn child. Like in the capitalist system of homogenized differentials, in the film's patriarchal order, the mother's body is treated as nothing more than a debased commodity. Indeed, whereas Immortan Joe defines the woman's womb as bare life, which he may sacrifice on a whim, he grants the unborn child full citizenship—surplus-value borne through the subjugation of its mother.

While much as been said about how the institution of motherhood places severe constraints upon mothers' bodies, rights, and labour, what is interesting and timely about *Fury Road* is how the film aligns these maternal restrictions with the ecological limits of late capitalism. In this way, the film visualizes what Jason Moore calls the "Capitalocene." According to Moore, we cannot understand the Anthropocene through the Cartesian split between labour and nature. Instead, the environmental crisis develops from the interlocking of two forms of labour-in-nature. The first involves paid work or the sphere of production; the second, symbolized by the Five Wives and the lactating mothers, is unpaid or cheap reproductive labour. For Moore, these two sets of labor generate a contradictory experience of time, wherein the reproductive time of life must serve the reproductive time of capital. Although many feminist scholars have established the centrality of this contradiction, for Moore, it is necessary to extend this analysis to explain the bio-social origins of the Anthropocene. It is not the case that the current ecological crisis is a matter of capitalism reaching the limits of nature; instead, the Anthropocene presupposes a social world organized around both the exploitation of ecological resources and abject labour.

"Cheap Nature" is the term Moore provides to theorize the ways capitalism pushes the limits of both unpaid domestic labour and cheap natural resources. Surplus value and further modes of accumulation demand extensive territories composed of cheap labour and energy. From this view, the ecological crisis emerges from the way capitalism has depleted both the differentials of nature and social reproduction. In *Fury Road*, the problem of Cheap Nature reaching its limits is seen in Immortan Joe's violent attempt at retaining control over the four flows (water, blood, milk, and guzzoline). Indeed, just as Moore draws attention to the failing ecological surplus (the idea that nature no longer yields returns on capitalistic investments), the film shows a nightmarish future that has run out of resources to extract value. It is only when the Five Wives escape the Citadel and challenge Immortan Joe's authority that the exploitative excesses of capitalism come undone. Without Cheap Nature, the Citadel's apparatus of power falters.

Mothering and Ecology without Nature

According to Stephen Maher, *Fury Road* functions as a classic western film. Like the western's captivity narrative, which hinges on the male hero's ability to rescue a "civilized" character from the clutches of barbarism, *Fury Road* traces Furiosa and Max's attempt at saving the Five Wives from the Citadel's apparatus of patriarchal power. Maher, however, only gets it half right. Claiming the goal of the captivity narrative involves returning "the captured people ... usually women ... home, to a place of purity and harmony," Maher misconstrues how the film parodies this desire to recover a pristine Mother Nature. This divergence from the captivity narrative is evidenced through Furiosa's mistaken belief in the Edenic possibilities of the Green Place, a matri-archal sanctuary in the desert, where women live in harmony with Mother Nature.

Throughout Western culture, two predominant Edenic recovery narratives have taken hold (Merchant). In one story, environmental progress depends upon humanity's ability to harness the power of science and technology to *construct* an Edenic paradise on earth. The second story tells of a monumental fall from grace, wherein humans have gradually severed themselves from a prehistoric time of immaculate nature. As Merchant writes: "Through these contrasting stories, we can see both progress and decline in different places at different times. Progressives want to continue the upward climb to recover the Garden of Eden by reinventing Eden on Earth, while environmentalists want to recover the original garden by restoring nature and creating sustain-ability" (3). It is the story of decline that pertains to Furiosa's faith in reaching the Green Place. Like many ecologists, Furiosa idealizes an Edenic form of untouched nature, in which women are not only free from servitude but retain a balanced and intimate relationship with Mother Nature. Merchant traces one version of this story to the work of the philosopher Max Oelschlaeger. According to Oelschlaeger, Paleolithic people did not distinguish between nature and culture but conducted themselves as part of a sustaining and all-encompassing natural whole. In this story of Edenic recovery, men and women came to live in peaceful harmony with each other and belonged to the sacred wholeness of the Great Mother (23).

If we believe Maher, the Green Place is the purified home the male hero reclaims for his civilized captives. However, what *Fury Road* reveals, and what Maher dismisses, is the futility of such an uncontaminated impression of nature. What Furiosa follows is an idealized image of Mother Nature, a maternal society that might have once existed but is beyond recovery. As McKenzie Wark writes, "There's no Eden, then, no green world. The goddess is dead and even the crones know it" ("Fury Road"). Although Furiosa mourns the loss of her birthplace (we learn that the Green Place deteriorated after the water became contaminated by toxic waste), she eventually realizes that Mother Nature is an ideological construct, a romanticized story that impedes her search for justice. Like the concept of Cheap Nature, which shows how the woman-nature dyad serves capitalism as an appropriative resource to create surplus value, the Green Place is an ideological mystification that normalizes women's nurturing and harmonious qualities. Furiosa's repudiation of the Green Place, however, does not mean that women cannot foster intimate relationships with the environment; what it shows instead is that home exists elsewhere, back in the city from where the captives fled, back to the contaminated spaces of carbon power. As Wark writes, "The task is not escape to the green world of fantasy. This is not a romantic story in any sense. The task is to remake the relation between superstructure and infrastructure. They have to return and take control of the apparatus of the four flows" ("Fury Road").

While critics like Wark rightfully point out *Fury Road*'s rejection of Edenic recovery narratives, another way to read Furiosa's denial of the Green Place entails a third story of nature offered by Merchant. This story begins in the 1990s with the arrival of chaos and complexity theory. Whereas many Edenic recovery narratives represent nature as a passive backdrop for human conquest or inert matter devoid of agency, in the complexity sciences, nature surfaces as an indeterminate, unpredictable, and unruly force that asserts its sovereignty over humans. As Merchant writes:

> The new approaches disrupted the idea of a balance of nature that humans could destroy but also restore. Humanity was not the

only major disturber of an evolved prehuman ecosystem. Natural disturbances, such as tornadoes, hurricanes, fires, and earthquakes could in an instant wipe out an old-growth forest, demolish a meadow, or redirect the meander of a river. Humanity was less culprit and more victim; nature more violent and less passive. Environmental history moved away from assigning all destructive change to humans and toward chance and contingency in nature. (6)

Today, Merchant's unruly view of nature carries over into a wide variety of contemporary philosophies, which understand nature neither as a romanticized sphere of nurturing plenitude nor as impotent matter tameable by human agency. Known as "dark ecology" (Morton), "ecology without nature" (Zizek), or "ecology against Mother Earth" (Wark), these reconceptualizations depend on a central contradiction of the Anthropocene: while humans have helped produce the Anthropocene, they cannot master or control it. Under this view, nature is a disunified and nonsovereign system that acts unpredictably (Latour). Humans cannot stand outside nature, since all things, including nature and culture, exist only through their relations with other things (Morton, *The Ecological Thought*). And life is not a stable and boundless reserve for humans but encompasses a streak of unimaginable catastrophes that defy all forms of mastery (Zizek, "Ecology without Nature").

For many material feminists, such as Elizabeth Grosz, Rosi Braidotti, and Stacey Alaimo, this troublesome nature presents fresh opportunities for blurring the misogynistic associations of women and nature. Unlike those who refuse to link women with nature, these material feminists embrace coalitions and kinships with nonhumans. As Haraway (*Staying with Trouble*) argues, becoming-with nonhumans does not reduce women or nature to rarified, passive, or victimized forms of materiality, nor do social constructionist critiques of the mother in Mother Nature mean that women can stand outside nature. Instead, the nature that emerges from the Anthropocene centres on what Brian Massumi calls the "Ex-Man"—a bodily materialism that subverts the sovereignty of humanist man by going through a process of genetic hybridization—mutations in which human matter meshes with other forms of bodily matter. As Rosi Braidotti writes:

This shift marks a sort of "anthropological exodus" from the dominant configurations of the human—a colossal hybridization of the species. The decentering of Anthropos challenges also the separation of bios, as exclusively human life, from zoe, the life of animals and nonhuman entities. What comes to the fore instead is a human-nonhuman continuum, which is consolidated by pervasive technological mediation. (26)

Despite many opportunities for promoting interspecies egalitarianism, a relational ontology of nature emphasizing openness, indeterminacy, and flux comes with many political risks. Braidotti fears that a commercialized approach to postanthropocentric life may also lead to postracial and postgender understandings of material difference. While many use Massumi's "Ex-Man" to critique hierarchies of power and promote social justice, in the hands of capitalism, postanthropocentric nature may depoliticize essential markers of difference. Seeking to put all forms of life in the service of capitalistic reproduction, technoscientific projects (e.g., DNA databases, patented lab animals, stem cell research, and genetically modified plants) often reduce life to abstract information, dematerialized codes, or rarefied data that "trade on life itself" (Braidotti 31). Although a nongendered conception of nature is welcomed, this commercialized disavowal of material difference may prove troubling for a feminist politics that seeks to uncover gender disparities. Perhaps Marcia Bjornerud's earlier call to appropriate images of Mother Nature "to unnerve the scientific community" (90) forms a timely appeal for us to reevaluate the posthuman.

Another problem with postanthropocentric interpretations of nature is that they may become the ground for the reclamation of men's sovereignty. According to Danielle Sands, this tendency runs throughout Latour's work on Gaia. For Sands, Latour's idea that humans and nature make up a system of reciprocal care practices can open a radical feminist politics of the Anthropocene. By politicizing Lovelock's earlier theories of Gaia as a self-regulating system that challenges man's sovereignty, Latour overcomes mechanistic notions of nature that treat it as an inexhaustible resource. Gaia is not an infinite possibility but a limited and parochial system that forces us earthbound. As he writes: "The great thing about Lovelock's Gaia is that it reacts, feels and might get rid of us, without being ontologically unified. It is not a superorganism endowed with any sort of unified agency. It is actually this total lack of unity that makes Gaia politically interesting. She is not a sovereign power lording it over us" ("Waiting for Gaia" 10).

By drawing upon the motherly qualities of Gaia, however, Latour produces an Anthropocene framework that "inclines us toward the replication of gender stereotypes" (288). For Sands, Latour's radical politics is compromised by his inability to explain how Gaia's nonsovereignty "could be translated into a form of agency that would evade recuperation by masculine sovereignty" (302). Indeed, while Gaia is represented as a dynamic force, Latour's string of maternal metaphors (Gaia is both frail and vengeful, both all-powerful and exhausted) converges with a long list of thinkers that either disparage the maternal powers of women or treat them as fragile creatures needing protection. Perhaps even more troubling for Sands is that Latour is unaware or dismisses the way disunity and nonsovereignty function as patriarchal hallmarks of women's inferiority, especially their so-called lack of bodily integrity. Comparing Latour's Gaia to Daniel Defoe's Robin Crusoe, Sands writes:

> Latour's aspirations of novelty … are actually anchored in the age-old dismissal of the female as supplementary, dispersed, and non-sovereign. Gaia is thus both the paradigm of dis-unified agency and, conveniently for Latour, the living deconstruction of the grand narrative of nature … The means by which woman is rendered absent are, however, comparable: in both cases, the association of woman with place ironically denies her a place from which to act. (297)

Returning to *Fury Road*'s denial of the Green Place, it is easy to see both the opportunities and pitfalls of postanthropocentric nature. Returning to the city, Furiosa takes charge of the four flows, creating a coalition with nature that gives agency to women. However, her journey away from Mother Nature just as readily forms the ground for the "recuperation of masculine sovereignty" (302). After all, it is Max who convinces Furiosa that Mother Nature does not exist and that justice can only come by returning to the city. And although Max leaves after Furiosa reclaims power, his gentle and nurturing role in helping the Five Wives questions the film's feminist politics. As McKenzie Wark writes, "This is not feminist cinema but a new kind of masculinist cinema—as far as it is prepared to compromise. Women (often 'middle aged') can figure things out for themselves, but with a little help from the universal donor, giving blood, not milk" ("Fury Road").

Children of Men and the Politics of Mothering

According to Slavoj Zizek, understanding *Children of Men's* geopolitics requires an anamorphic perspective. For Zizek, the foreground of the film tells the superficial story of Theo's (Clive Owen) spiritual journey from political apathy to citizen engagement. As the viewer learns in the opening voiceover, the collapse of society coincides with an infertility crisis. With the last recorded birth taking place eighteen years earlier, the film presents a dystopian world, whose true horror results from a "slow death" (Fukuyama). Although most postapocalyptic worlds burn up in a fury of instantaneous violence, the one presented in *Children of Men* is even more terrifying, since it lingers on without a future to give it meaning. For Theo, who already lost a child, the global infertility crisis results in social suicide: apathetic, depressed, and engulfed in alcoholism, Theo symbolizes the impotence of a universal subjectivity about to come to an end (Chaudhary).

For Zizek, the film's real politics does not occur at this level of narration. Even though the movie focuses on Theo's quest to help Kee, a pregnant refugee, reach the Human Project, for Zizek, everything of value takes place obliquely in the background: global infertility and the protagonist's search for atonement make sense only against the backdrop of a capitalistic system that seeks to erase human history. No doubt, the film displays a rich tapestry of political imagery. From images of the detention and torture of immigrants to scenes involving religious fanatics, angry protests, and piles of burning bodies, the film is notable for its dire depiction of the current state of things. However, this is far from the film's only site of meaning. I contend that instead of emphasizing the background, we should take the foreground seriously; put another way, I propose a new anamorphic reading, one where the essential backdrop is not the social disparity lurking behind the scenes but the maternal body that sets in motion the film's narrative journey. I hope to venture beyond Zizek's symbolic reading of infertility by postulating that Kee's pregnancy forms the central axes of meaning. The maternal crisis does not merely represent either the defeat of history or the decadence of Western capitalism; instead, it shows the role caretaking plays in creating new kinships and communities.

By reducing women's infertility to abstract symbols of human hope and despair, Zizek neglects to see how both experiences materialize in everyday practices, such as the ongoing labour bound up with maternal care. Even suggesting that Kee's maternal experience is not the real subject of the film contributes to a long-standing tradition of negating mothers' material realities, whose performance of everyday care becomes nothing more than inconsequential filler. This tendency to erase maternal labour is clear in Zizek's ideological reading of Theo's best friend, Jasper (Michael Caine). A former activist and political cartoonist, Jasper is shown spending his last days living off the grid as a "Granola Guy." For Zizek, Jasper's ultraleftist ideology represents an obscene and impotent infantilism, a radical politics that complements rather than critiques capitalism. Although this may be true, what Zizek fails to apprehend is that Jasper is also a caring character, who more than once reveals the labour required for participating in social forms of care. Jasper is what I would call a postapocalyptic version of Sara Ruddick's maternal thinker. He is someone who takes part in the ongoing protection, nurturance, and care of others. Not only does he take special care of his incapacitated wife, but he also acts as a father figure to Theo; likewise, when Theo helps Kee reach the Human Project, Jasper comes to their rescue, providing shelter and safe passage. Jasper is even willing to sacrifice his life so Theo and Kee may continue their journey unharmed. Thus, by taking responsibility for the care of others, Jasper provides a cinematic version of what Bernice Fisher and Joan Tronto call "the core components of care." Care, they write, is an "activity that includes everything that we do to maintain, continue, and repair our 'world' so that we can live in it as well as possible. That world includes our bodies, ourselves, and our environment, all of which we seek to interweave in a complex, life-sustaining web" (40).

While Zizek devotes little attention to the maternal figure, other critics manage to highlight Kee's status as a Black mother: Zahid Chaudhary views Kee's fertility through the "race/reproduction bind," whereby Kee's pregnant body activates a chain of racial stereotypes, from her excessive animal-like fertility to her status as the new African Eve. For Karima K. Jeffrey, Kee signifies the Biblical character Hagar, a Black surrogate mother who never acts on her own but requires the paternal protection of others. Sarah Trimble reads Kee through Agamben's biopolitics, a move that envisions her pregnancy as a form of bare life tied to modern colonialism and slavery. Finally, Nicole Sparling uses Lauren Berlant's theories about nationalism and female reproduction to show how the rights of the fetus denigrate Kee's status as a mother.

Although these diverse readings of Black maternity open the film to a broader politics linking issues of materiality, race, postcolonial nationalism, and motherhood, they all reduce the mother figure to an institutional framework reinforced by patriarchy.

Given Kee's position as one of cinema's few Black maternal characters, it is surprising that these critics do not draw upon the rich body of literature that regards mothering as a resource of power for Black women. From Patricia Hill Collins's work on Black standpoint theory and bell hooks' reconception of home as a place of maternal resistance to Toni Morrison's belief that mothering serves to empower children, theories of Black mothering often focus on positions of power rather than servitude. In these understandings of maternal thinking, not only do practices of care preserve and empower future children, they also construct models of parenting that replace the heteronormative family with a communal system prioritizing collective knowledge and kinships. To draw upon this view of Black maternity, I offer an oppositional, counterreading of *Children of Men*. This perspective does not deny these other maternal readings of Kee (the film is not by any means a utopia of Black motherhood); instead, I look to salvage moments of care in the movie to reinstate the neglected and disavowed importance of mothering as forms of political resistance.

To recover an empowering conception of the maternal, I start at the ending. For many critics, it is in the final scenes that the film explicitly uses the mother-child dyad to mark a hopeful image of the future. It is also here that most critics deny Kee's role as a mother and maternal thinker. After escaping the refugee camp, Theo, Kee, and baby Dylan sail out to sea in search of the elusive Human Project. Moments before the ship rescues them, Theo dies, leaving Kee to fend for herself. As the ship peers through the fog, the film shows Kee consoling her crying child; while singing a soft lullaby, she rocks the baby and proclaims, "We are safe." As the film closes, the words "Children of Men" appear against a black screen. We then hear the cheerful sounds and playful screams of children. In contrast to the film's final images of a grey and foreboding sea, the sounds evoke the simple joys of frolicking children, those endless summer evenings where for a few moments time stands still.

For Chaudhary, the key to unlocking the film's use of allegory to understand how materiality produces racial difference begins here in the jostling sounds of children's babble. Since the sounds do not yet form recognizable words, the children's voices belong to an inchoate material base from which language will eventually emerge and try to master a world of alterity. The sounds are, for Chaudhary, a place of utopia—a pregnant moment of prelinguistic materiality that precedes the film's visualization of racial difference. The problem with Chaudhary's reading of this scene is that he understands materiality only as a matter of language. He fails to see how the children's joyful sounds result from another kind of materiality: the labour bound up with practices of motherly care. It does not dawn on Chaudhary that the condition of possibility for children's laughter is the physical labour of some mother, who works towards the demand of fostering children's growth (Ruddick). Nor does he contend with the possibility that language and thinking are themselves born from acts of care that bring people in close contact with the material world. As Ruddick writes: "Caretakers are immersed in the materials of the physical world. The physical phenomena of human and other bodies must be interpreted in relation to the demands of caretaking. It is not useful to abstract to air, earth, water, and fire, let alone electrons. Whether care workers are cleaning toilets or toilet training children ... they depend upon a practical knowledge of the material world" (130).

This rejection of maternal labour also emerges in Sarah Trimble's account of Kee's lullaby. While Kee sings in the Ga language, Trimble provides an English translation: "Don't cry, don't cry, don't cry for someone to look in your mouth / A gold nugget is in your mouth / Don't cry for someone to look in your mouth" (259). For Trimble, even though the song is meant to soothe the newborn, the lyrics betray the reassuring tonality of the singing mother. By referring to a violent colonial past, the song undermines the hopefulness of Kee's role as the future of humanity. As Trimble writes, "Even as Kee comforts Dylan and assures her that they are 'safe now,' the lullaby locates a precious metal within the infant and evokes a history of imperial violence on the Gold Coast, thereby constructing Dylan's body as contested terrain" (259).

Trimble's account of how the lullaby's language conjures a violent history of colonial extraction complements Chaudhary's account of how language tries to master alterity by demarcating a hierarchy of physical markers of difference. I argue that focusing exclusively on the lyrics denies the motherly protection evidenced in the scene. Like Chaudhary's erasure of the materiality of maternal labour, Trimble rejects the protective and nurturing significance of the song. For the child, what matters is not the lyrics but the sonic tonality and tenor of the mother's singing voice. For the child, the lullaby functions as what Lacan calls an "acoustic mirror," a maternal voice that envelopes the newborn in intimacy and pleasure (Silverman). As Lawrence Kramer writes, "The child understands the song—correctly—as full of love and happiness only because she does not understand the song at all" (304).

Another hopeful interpretation of these scenes comes from Zizek, who maintains that the future of humanity lies in the boat's rootlessness. Unlike the divisive ground of the nation-state, which approaches the global crisis by policing the boundaries between legitimate and illegitimate bodies, the ocean is an amorphous place of indeterminate possibility. By taking to the water, Kee and Dylan sever their roots with the past, making available a renewed space of collective optimism. In her reading of the boat, Trimble takes Zizek to task, arguing that his symbolic interpretation of Kee's voyage elides the ocean's historical legacy as a space of colonial violence. For Trimble, Kee's status as a stateless Black mother conjures a fraught history of transatlantic slavery, a practice that saw countless Black mothers left to drown at sea. From a colonial perspective, then, Zizek's notion of oceanic freedom works only by denying how the transatlantic helped construct a version of European sovereignty dependent on the trade of "capital, bodies, [and] babies" (Weinbaum 2). Thus, instead of the sea offering a safe place for mother and child, the ship's arrival evokes the "drowning grounds of the Atlantic" (258), an oceanic haunting that questions Kee's maternal powers of renewal.

Again, both perspectives reject Kee's experience as a maternal thinker. Insisting that her fertility stands as either an abstract symbol of hope or an imprisoned form of bare life, both critics fail to see how acts of mothering create collective resources for forging ahead in new material kinships. By focusing only on the rootlessness of the ocean, Zizek transforms the boat into a fetish object that disavows the web of labour intertwined with care practices. Zizek never thinks about the collective work involved in procuring the boat; he never considers the assemblage of caretakers that provide Kee safe passage; he never attends to the material conditions required for the safe delivery of Kee's child.

Taking the maternal ethics of the film seriously, I claim the message of hope lives in relations of care—the laying down of roots, however temporary, for protecting life. In place of the rootless boat, I suggest Haraway's (*Staying with Trouble*) string figures as a more promising way to conceive the film's politics of collective possibility. No single act or actor enables Kee to arrive at the Human Project. Instead, many acts of giving and taking, multiple moments of passing forth, create the web of care required to repair and maintain the world. However, we should not confuse this family of caretakers with traditional kinships. The laying down of roots does not produce a molar order of male paternity or a heightening of national bloodlines. By sacrificing his life for Kee, Theo does not become the sacrificial head of household, whose protection ensures the future of humanity (Marcus O'Donnell calls Theo a midwife to Kee's baby.) Rather, Kee's mothering sets in motion what Gilles Deleuze and Felix Guattari call "the art of fabulation." Like Deleuze and Guattari's poet, Kee is a caretaker who "lets loose molecular populations hoping this will sow the seeds of, or even engender, the people to come, that these populations will pass into a people to come, open a cosmos" (345). When Zizek talks of the ocean as a place without roots, he forgets that Kee's entire journey forms a cosmos of new kinships, a fragile community of caretakers. All the elemental people that help Kee—this unlikely band of dissociated caretakers—are nothing if not a depopulated people that mesh into mobile assemblages. A true oddkin, they recall what Haraway (*Simians, Cyborgs, and Women*) calls denatured engagements: temporary and mobile coalitions based not on blood bonds or identify but affinity and choice.

Although Trimble's historical perspective avoids Zizek's abstraction, her account of the mother-child dyad cannot break free from the institutional framework that sees motherhood as only a site of subjugation. She never considers how the ocean also serves as a vital space of maternal fabulation. For Michel Serres, the sea is abundantly maternal:

> The living sea, vital, vivifying, first mother of the living species, the maternal sea, soft as a baby's skin, without a ripple, rocked in the calm after the storm, flowering breast, uterus, fertile womb, generous source of fecundity, parturient and nourishing to the point of repletion ... the primeval Eve sea from whose wombs we all came, seaweed, plants and animals, bacteria and mammals, reptiles and whales, even humans, billions, then millions of years ago. (10)

If Serres's admiration of the maternal sea seems too fantastical, one could also consider the maternal function of the ocean in Afrofuturism—a movement that contests colonial knowledge through science fiction and speculative thinking. In the music of the Detroit-based band Drexciya, for example, a counterhistorical discourse emerges that envisions the ocean as the site of an African American utopia that forms under the sea. In this story of maternal hope, the group imagines that all the mothers and unborn children who drowned at sea survive and create their own Black Atlantis. As Melody Jue writes, throughout a long genealogy of Afrofuturist speculations the ocean emerges "as both a means of cultural survival and a catalyst for future evolution, a familiar alterity" (176). I frame Kee's experience at sea through this counter-discourse of oceanic fabulation. While there is no guarantee that the Human Project will provide her safe passage, Kee's willingness to protect and preserve her child embodies what Sara Ruddick calls "maternal cheerfulness." To be cheerful, Ruddick writes, "means to respect chance, limit, and imperfection and still act as if it is possible to keep children safe. Cheerfulness is a matter-of-fact willingness to accept having given birth, to start and to start over again, to welcome a future despite conditions of oneself, one's society and nature that may be reasons for despair" (74). To start and start over again despite a world of despair—this is the maternal politics of *Children of Men*. It is not the abstract symbolism of Zizek, nor is it the biopolitics offered by Trimble; it is a material way of creating ongoing kinships that find life in the ruins of environmental precarity.

Conclusion: Which Stories? Or Cinema in the Age of the Anthropocene

In the past decade, such documentary films as *An Inconvenient Truth*, *Cowspiracy*, *Chasing Ice*, *Great Warming*, and *Trashed* have become prime vehicles for addressing global environmental issues. Although the worldwide reach of these films has helped ecological activists spread their messages about the planet's degradation, these stories rarely acknowledge the complex and contradictory role gender figures within environmental advocacy and representations of nature. In this chapter, I argue that the genre offering the most critical perspective on ecological representations of gender is the postapocalyptic disaster film. Through analyzing *Mad Max: Fury Road* and *Children of Men*, I show how environmental disaster films link the earth's degradation to women's fertility—a practice calling for a maternal framework to deconstruct the metaphorical uses of the mother-nature dyad. Through the Maternalocene, I call attention to the need to think about the Anthropocene through two interrelated meanings of motherhood. First, as seen in the film *Fury Road*, a feminist politics for the Anthropocene requires paying attention to how ecological crises converge with climate injustices, such as the exhausting of both cheap nature and unpaid domestic labour. Second, such films as *Children of Men* show how mothering can also serve as a resource for empowerment and provide an ethics of care that may help in the maintenance and reparation of the world.

Endnotes

1. The Anthropocene is a geological term referring to the possibility that we are living in a new geological time period (the age of man). Although the term has a specific meaning in geology, the Anthropocene also functions as a broad concept bringing together multiple environmental issues, from climate change and species extinction to rising sea levels and the acidification of the ocean. I keep the latter meaning throughout this chapter.

Works Cited

After Earth. Directed by M. Night Shyamalan, Sony Pictures, 2013.

An Inconvenient Truth. Directed by Davis Guggenheim, Paramount Classics, 2006.

Alaimo, Stacey. "Your Shell on Acid: Material Immersion, Anthropocene Dissolves." *Anthropocene Feminism*, edited by Richard Grushin, University of Minnesota Press, 2017, pp. 89-120.

Avatar. Directed by James Cameron, 20th Century Fox, 2009.

Bales, Kevin. *Disposable People: New Slavery in the Global Economy*. University of California Press, 2012.

Beasts of the Southern Wild. Directed by Benh Zeitlin, Fox Searchlight, 2012.

Bonneuil, Christophe, and Jean-Baptiste Fressoz. *The Shock of the Anthropocene*. Verso, 2015.

Bjornerud, Marcia. "Gaia: Gender and Scientific Representations of the Earth." *NWSA* Journal, vol. 9, no. 3, 1997, pp. 89-106.

Braidotti, Rosi. "Four Theses on Poshuman Feminism." *Anthropocene Feminism*, edited by Richard Grusin, University of Minnesota Press, 2017, pp. 21-48.

Brassier, Ray. *Nihil Unbound: Enlightenment and Extinction.* Palgrave MacMillan, 2007.

Bressler, Nancy, and Lara Lengel. "Mothering in Dystopia: Lone Parenting in a Post Apocalyptic World." *Motherhood and Single-Lone Parenting: A Twenty-First Century Perspective*, edited by Maki Motapanyane, Demeter Press, 2016, pp. 19-52.

Chasing Ice. Directed by Jeff Orlowski, National Geographic, 2012.

Collins, Patricia Hill. *Black Feminist Thought: Knowledge, Consciousness, and the Politics of Empowerment.* Routledge, 2008.

Cowspiracy: The Sustainability Secret. Directed by Kip Anderson and Keegan Kuhn, Appian Way Productions, 2014.

Children of Men. Directed by Alfonso Cuarón, Universal Pictures, 2006.

Chaudhary, Zahid R. "Humanity Adrift: Race, Materiality, and Allegory in Alfonso Cuarón's Children of Men." *Camera Obscura*, vol. 24, no. 3, 2009, pp. 73-109.

Clover, Joshua, and Juliana Spahr. "Gender Abolition and Ecotone War." *Anthropocene Feminism*, edited by Richard Grushin, University of Minnesota Press, 2017, pp. 291-311.

Colebrook, Claire. "Fragility, Globalism, and the End of the World." *YouTube*, uploaded by Yale University, 8 Nov. 2017, www.youtube. com/watch?v=_lOQpyu84WA. Accessed 26 May 2020.

Deleuze, Gilles and Felix Guartti. *A Thousand Plateaus: Capitalism and Schizophrenia.* University of Minnesota Press, 1987.

District 9. Directed by Neill Blomkamp, Sony Pictures/Screen Gems, 2009.

Drexciya. *The Quest.* Submerge, 1997.

Fisher, Bernice, and Joan C. Tronto. "Toward a Feminist Theory of Care." *Circles of Care: Work and Identity in Women's Lives*, edited by Emily K. Abel and Margaret K. Nelson, SUNY Press, 1990, pp. 36-54.

Franklin, Leanne, and John Cromby. "Everyday Fear: Parenting and Childhood in a Culture of Fear." *The Many Forms of Fear, Horror and Terror*, edited by Leanne Franklin and Ravenel Richardson, Inter-Disciplinary Press, 2009, pp. 161-174.

Fukuyama, Francis. "Francis Fukuyama Explains Why Children of Men Is So Great." *YouTube*, uploaded by Slate, 17 Oct. 2016, www.youtube.com/watch?v=03SrMeLmOUc. Accessed 26 May 2020.

Geostorm. Directed by Dean Devlin, Warner Bros. Pictures, 2017.

Ghosh, Amitav. *The Great Derangement: Climate Change and the Un-thinkable*. University of Chicago Press, 2016.

Gravity. Directed by Alfonso Cuarón, Warner Bros. Pictures, 2013.

Great Warming. Directed by Michael Taylor, Stonehaven, 2006.

Haraway, Donna. *Simians, Cyborgs, and Women: The Reinvention of Nature*. Routledge, 1991.

Haraway, Donna. *Staying with Trouble: Making Kin in the Chthulucene*. Duke University Press, 2016.

Haraway, Donna. "Situated Knowledges: The Science Question in Feminism and the Privilege of Partial Perspective." *Feminist Studies*, vol. 14, no. 3, 1988, pp. 575-99.

Homo Sapiens. Directed by Nikolaus Geyrhalter, Kimstim Films, 2016.

hooks, bell. *Feminist Theory: From Margin to Center*. South End Press, 2000.

I am Legend. Directed by Francis Lawrence, Warner Bros. Pictures, 2007.

Jeffrey, Karima. "Mother of a New World? Stereotypical Representa-tions of Black Women in Three Post-apocalyptic Films." *Journal of Feminist Scholarship*, vol. 6, no. 6, 2014, pp. 1-12.

Jue, Melody. "Intimate Objectivity: On Nnedi Okorafor's Oceanic Afrofuturism." *Women's Studies Quarterly*, vol. 45, nos. 1 & 2, 2017, pp. 171-188.

Kramer, Lawrence. "Beyond Words and Meaning: An Essay on Songfulness." *Word and Music Studies: Defining the Field*, edited by Walter Bernhart, Steven Paul Scher, and Werner Wolf, Rodopi, 1999, pp. 303-320.

Latour, Bruno. *Facing Gaia: Eight Lectures on the New Climatic Regime*. Polity, 2017.

Latour, Bruno. "Waiting for Gaia. Composing the Common World through Arts and Politics." A Lecture at the Institut Français du Royaume-Uni, *Bruno Latour*, Nov. 2011, www.bruno-latour.fr/sites/default/files/124-GAIA-LONDON-SPEAP_0.pdf. Accessed 26 May 2020.

Lepawsky. Josh, "The Wake of the Anthropocene." *Techniques & Culture*, vols. 65-66, 2016, journals.openedition.org/tc/7792. Accessed 26 May 2020.

Logsdon-Conradsen, Susan. "From Maternalism to Activist Mothering: The Evolution of Mother Activism in the United States Environmental Movement." *Journal of the Motherhood Initiative for Research and Community Involvement*, vol. 2, no. 1, 2000, pp. 9-36.

Lovelock, James. *The Revenge of Gaia: Earth's Climate Crisis & The Fate of Humanity.* Basic Books, 2007.

Maher, Stephen. "Mad Max and the End of the World." Jacobin. 26 May 2015, www.jacobinmag.com/2015/05/mad-max-fury-road-review/. Accessed 26 May 2020.

Mad Max: Fury Road. Directed by George Miller, Warner Bros., 2015.

Massumi, Brian. "Requiem for Our Prospective Dead (Toward a Participatory Critique of Capitalist Power)." *Deleuze and Guattari: New Mappings in Politics, Philosophy, and Culture,* edited by Eleanor Kaufman and Kevin John Heller, University of Minnesota Press, 1998, pp. 40-64.

Massumi, Brian. *The Politics of Everyday Fear.* The University of Minnesota Press, 1993.

Merchant, Carolyn. *Reinventing Eden: The Fate of Nature in Western Culture.* Routledge, 2004.

Moore, Jason. *Capitalism in the Web of Life: Ecology and the Accumulation of Capital.* Verso, 2015.

Morton, Timothy. *Humankind: Solidarity with Nonhuman People.* Verso, 2017.

Morton, Timothy. *Dark Ecology: For a Logic of Future Coexistence.* Columbia University Press, 2016.

Morton, Timothy. *Hyperobjects: Philosophy and Ecology After the End of the World.* University of Minnesota Press, 2013.

Morton, Timothy. *The Ecological Thought.* Harvard University Press, 2012.

Nixon, Rob. *Slow Violence and the Environmentalism of the Poor.* Harvard University Press, 2011.

O'Donnell, Marcus. "Children of Men's Ambient Apocalyptic Visions." *Journal of Religion and Popular Culture*, vol. 27, no. 1, 2015, pp. 16-30.

Okja. Directed by Bong Joon Ho, Netflix, 2017.

O'Reilly, Andrea. *From Motherhood to Mothering: The Legacy of Adrienne Rich's* Of Woman Born. SUNY Press, 2004.

Parikka, Jussi. "New Materialism as Media Theory: Medianatures and Dirty Matter." *Communication and Critical/Cultural Studies*, vol. 9, no. 1, 2012, pp. 95-100.

Pirici, Andrea, and Raluca Voinea. "Manifesto for the Gynecene—Sketch of a New Geological Era." *Tranzit*, ro.tranzit.org/file/MANIFESTO-for-the-Gynecene.pdf. Accessed 26 May 2002.

Prometheus. Directed by Ridley Scott, 20th Century Fox, 2012.

Rich, Adrienne. *Of Woman Born: Motherhood as Experience and Institution.* Norton, 1986.

Roach, Catherine. "Loving Your Mother: On the Woman-Nature Relation." *Hypatia*, vol. 6, no. 1, 1991, pp. 46-59.

Ruddick, Sara. *Maternal Thinking: Toward a Politics of Peace.* Beacon Press, 1989.

Sands, Danielle. "Gaia, Gender, and Sovereignty in the Anthropocene." *philoSOPHIA*, vol. 5, no. 2, 2015, pp. 287-307.

Serres, Michel. *Biogea.* Translated by Burks Randolph, Univocal Publishing, 2012.

Sheldon, Rebekah. *The Child to Come: Life After the Human Catastrophe.* University of Minnesota Press, 2016.

Silverman, Kaja. *The Acoustic Mirror.* Indiana University Press, 1988.

Sobchack, Vivian. "Bringing It All Back Home: Family Economy and Generic Exchange." *The Dread of Difference*, edited by Barry Keith Grant, University of Texas Press, 1996, pp. 171-191.

Snowpiercer. Directed by Bong Joon Ho, Radius-TWC, 2014.

Sparling, Nicole. "Without a Conceivable Future: Figuring the Mother in Alfonso Cuarón's Children of Men." *Frontiers: A Journal of Women Studies*, vol. 35, no. 1, 2014, pp. 160-180.

Stengers, Isabelle. *In Catastrophic Times: Resisting the Coming Barbarism.* Open Humanities Press, 2015.

Thacker, Eugene. *In the Dust of This Planet: Horror of Philosophy.* John Hunt Publishing, 2011. Kindle Edition.

The Book of Eli. Directed by Albert Hughes and Allen Hughes, Warner Bros. Pictures, 2010.

The Day after Tomorrow. Directed by Roland Emmerich, 20th Century Fox, 2004.

The Handmaid's Tale. Created by Bruce Miller, Hulu, 2017.

The Lottery. Created by Timothy J. Sexton, Lifetime, 2014.

The Road. Directed by Javier Aguirresarobe and John Hillcoat, The Weinstein Co./Dimension, 2009.

Trashed. Directed by Candida Brady, Blenheim Films, 2012.

Trimble, Sarah. "Maternal Back/grounds in Children of Men: Notes toward an Arendtian Biopolitics." *Biopolitics, Science Fiction Film and Television,* vol. 4, no. 2, 2011, pp. 249-70.

Wark, McKenzie. "Fury Road." *Public Seminar,* 22 May 2015, www.publicseminar.org/2015/05/fury-road/. Accessed 26 May 2020.

Wark, McKenzie. *Molecular Red: Theory for the Anthropocene.* London, Verso, 2015.

Wark, McKenzie. "Anthropo{mise-en-s}cène." *Public Seminar,* December 10, 2014, www.publicseminar.org/2014/12/anthropomise- en-scene/. Accessed 26 May 2020.

Weinbaum, Alys Eve. *Wayward Reproductions: Genealogies of Race and Nation in Transatlantic Modern Thought.* Duke University Press, 2004.

Weisman, Allan. *The World Without Us.* Harper Perennial, 2008.

Yates, Michelle. "Re-casting nature as feminist space in Mad Max: Fury Road." *Science Fiction Film and Television,* vol. 10, no. 3, 2017, pp. 353-370.

Zizek, Slavoj. "Zizek on Children of Men." *YouTube,* uploaded by Anthony Arroyo, 9 Sept. 2007, www.youtube.com/watch?v=pbgrw NP_gYE. Accessed 26 May 2020.

Zizek, Slavoj. "Ecology without Nature." *YouTube,* uploaded by mboudour, 5 Oct. 2007, www.youtube.com/watch?time_continue= 2&v=NyzTif1QJjA. Accessed 26 May 2020.

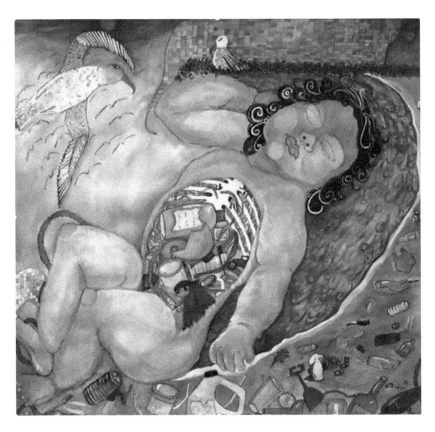

Baby New Year Plastic World

Dara Herman Zierlein

Chapter Six

Poems

Josephine Savarese

Restoring Cat Island, Louisiana[1]

The remains of Cat Island

A dream: A skiff filled with wrongfully convicted women
Arrives after the
BP Deepwater Horizion oil spill
Wearing sunglasses, steel toed
Boots, graying prison garb with
Torn, empty pockets.
Women embark on two tiny strips of sand and shell
What is left of the miles-long island
Smaller than a solitary cell

Muscled arms
Pull mangrove stumps
Into full trees with bare hands
That never bleed.

Resurrect the once teaming
Rookery, uncover withered
Spoonbills lost in bowls.
Build nests with sticks
cigarette butts, broken teeth
and pelican bills
Throw tar balls
For imaginary dogs
Chewing on ibis
Bones.
Ice their hearts
In beer coolers
Stuffed with
Eyeless fish
Drunk on Budweiser.

Jail ink and life
Sentences fade in
sub-tropical heat
no limit on yard
time.

Shovel for roots
Where coastal birds
Imprinted, returned.

Feathery offspring
born knowing freedom
Is a wingspan.

Use the booms as
Beach toys, floating
empty promises
beyond the forever
blackened sheen

Wash down oil slicked
Herons hoping for
Another chance,
Huddle in disgrace.
Praying in bird talk
For exoneration.

Tammy Marquardt Fumes at British Petroleum
(after the Oil Spill)

Reaches way down
Through the cell
Bars to take hold
Of an oil slicked
Pelican

Only six months off
The endangered
Species list

Swears so
Loudly

Even the
Roseate
Spoonbill
Carcasses
Blush.

Tammy Marquardt Becomes a Bullfighter in Plaquemines Parish, Louisiana

Strides into the ring
Matadora finery, head high
Mauve *traje de luces*

Sword a sorcerer's
Wand transforms bull
Into a Seaside Sparrow

Flies upward,
Away,
All the while,
singing.

Tammy bows.
Crowd, hungry for
Blood, boos.

Sparrow flutters
overhead.
Tammy exits.

All the while,
Humming the
tune of the
Dead ocean.

Endnotes

1. Describing the island as it was before the oil spill, local government official, P.J. Hahn offered this perspective:

    In 2010 prior to the oil spill, this was a pristine island with about 8 foot mangroves. It was roughly around 5 and a half, almost six acres. This was ideal nesting ground for migratory birds in the wintertime looking for places to nest for the spring. When the oil spill hit these little islands were here to greet the oil. US wildlife and fishery studies show that chicks when they're born will imprint to these islands so every year they return to the same place they were born to breed and nest again. The study also shows that when the birds come back here if the island gone, they don't go off and breed somewhere else, they just don't breed. So, we're losing generation after generation of birds. ("The Forgotten Island").

Works Cited

"The Forgotten Island Destroyed by the Gulf Oil Spill," *Waking Times*, 5 May, 2017, www.wakingtimes.com/2017/05/05/the-island-thal-disinegrated/. Accessed 31 May 2020.

Chapter Seven

Excerpt from *the Bones*

Laura Wythe

TinTin slowed down and turned into the long laneway of the family farm. She pinched him on the neck so hard that he stopped. A sudden flash of memories washed up inside her and were tumbling over her heart like polished stones.

"I've been imprinted too."

TinTin reached up and took her hand down, and held it. They sat, each with their own thoughts, the car windows steaming up from their breathing.

For Clem, the sudden pang had come on seeing the five-seated glider with its faded olefin cushions on the front porch. A five-year-old girl had waited there for sleep to come. She'd counted shooting stars from the tip of her grandfather's finger. When cool air seeped up through the spaces in the porch floor boards, she had curled her legs up on the cushions, leaning closer into her grandfather's lean body. He scooped her onto his lap. She struggled against the warmth and comfort to keep her head up, heavy as it was with sleep. Finally, she let it fall against his chest, wedging it under his chin so that she could watch the lane for her parents to come. They had promised to return that evening. In her sleepiness, she confused the headlights of her parents' car sparking down the lane with the transient flashes of the meteor shower that streaked the sky above.

Another stone. A seven-year-old girl walked past where the car was idling. She carried mail up the lane to the house, tall corn on one side, pasture on the other. Her grandmother stood up from weeding the garden to wave. Onions and cabbage grew on the slope towards the river. Sweet carrots hid beneath the black, mysterious soil, the result of some agreement her grandmother had made with them, she'd thought.

Then a ten-year-old looked out from the lantern of the widow's walk, wondering whose trucks were parked in the lane. Most days, all she saw were fields filled with a maze of paths that must be seen from above to be understood. She had to memorize them or she would run blind. She drew secret maps of the shortcuts, the cul-de-sacs, the places where men who smelled of peppermint and machine oil might gather. Those men had a too easy tease ready on their lips. They were about to take the hay off the front field.

"Whose boy is this?"

"It must be another one of the Dolsen boys."

"Sure is growing up fine."

"He'll be big enough to help with the corn by fall, for sure."

A round of winking made it worse. The ten-year-old girl stood her ground in the field, the message from her grandmother delivered. She knew to wait politely, that she was expected to wait for the reward. Her grandfather pulled a tin of mints from his shirt pocket and offered "the boy" one, so proud she belonged to him.

By the time she was twelve years old, there were different errands. The attic and windows in the widow's walk, which had given her a map to the farm, became a source of pain. She did not share her mother's love of old things. Yet her grandmother used the same tactics on Clem, as she had on Catherine, to indoctrinate Clem into the past. Suddenly her grandmother needed a parade of mothballed history.

"These old legs don't do stairs as well as they once did. Perhaps, Clementyne, you'd take this key and see if the *name-that-item* is in the *name-that-colour* trunk."

The twelve-year-old opened trunks with the care of a snake handler. Pinched fingers picked out lace, wool, china, tin toys. She spit with anger at the tiny spiders that bit and left itchy welts, squealed at the sight of earwigs that raised their pinchers when their nests were disturbed. Photo albums, photos framed, silverware and cups, and medical devices—including enema bags and rubber doughnuts for the sufferers of haemorrhoids—required more fingers. The books. She hated searching the book trunks. Small grey moths flew out. Their sticky cocoons bound the pages together. The smell. They smelled of yellow, wrinkled old stories that should have stayed locked up in trunks forever. And more teasing.

"Hasn't she found his bones up there yet?"

By her fourteenth summer, the past had been conquered, and she was allowed downstairs again. The kitchen door had a lovely weight as it swung shut on the dining room where working men ate huge dinners at noon. She'd swing the door open and confidently set down platters of meat and bowls of vegetables, enough to fill the men after a long morning cutting hay, or taking off the wheat. Silence reigned while they ate the main course. Conversation came with dessert and coffee—grunts about the weather, figuring and questioning about the neighbours' plantings, silences ending with "Jeezus!" followed by the clatter of cutlery. They saw her as a woman, and they must have thought long and hard on suitable topics to bring up when she entered.

"Hargrave," a neighbour would say, a honeyed innocence in his voice as she remembered it now. "It's too bad you don't open that field to the south. Then we could get Jackson's binder down there."

"South is still too wet in June. Daddy said he would lose the binder down there, don't think he hasn't thought of going down himself."

"Oh, *Daddy* has? You don't say?" The sun-burnt men laughed, poking fun at the seventeen-year-old at the table, so that he turned even redder in front of the fourteen-year-old girl who served their dinner.

The swinging door rocked back and forth between rooms, then quieted. Clem ate at the kitchen table with her grandmother.

"They can shout if they need anything else."

Poor Hargrave was sent to the kitchen to ask for more sugar, poking his head through the door and offering the empty bowl, but not daring to step in despite the men's encouragement.

"Go on, she won't bite."

Soon enough, they went back to work. Her grandmother put the white tablecloth into Clem's hands and sent her out to shake the crumbs. Sparrows fought over them before they hit the ground. The birds had to be quick. Not all the barn cats were out chasing deer mice in the newly cut fields.

"Okay?" asked TinTin.

Clem started to say yes, but then the hardest memory in her life tumbled through her heart, a large polished stone the colour of jet. A memory of the good parlour. Her grandfather's accident. He had lived in that room for three weeks after the tractor fell onto him, propped up in a hospital bed by the west window where he could see the bare branches of the sassafras bush, and look up past the branches of a sugar maple to the sky and the stars at night. His body was injured beyond repair. It only needed time to learn how to die. At dusk, moths pelted the window. The lamps were draped with scarves.

An arm chair was set beside the bed, always occupied by a knitter, a reader of scripture or almanacs, a scribe to the lists of business that cultivated her grandfather's mind. He spoke slowly to those in the chair and listened to them as though he had all the time in the world. Clem took the late shift. She could hear her mother and grandmother, the visiting great aunts and uncles and cousins tossing on the bedsprings upstairs. In the night, no one came down to interfere with her *impractical* sketching. Her grandfather didn't mind the reading light behind the back of the arm chair as long as it didn't cast a glare on the west window. The girl chewed on the ends of her hair, looking for things to draw in the shadows cast by the lamplight, darkly smudging in the radio cabinet, the sideboard, the over-sized sofa, a bear's head mounted on a heraldic shield. Her grandfather dozed and woke. He asked her to draw Jack, dead for twenty years. She sketched the dog from her memory of photos—sleeping, eating, jumping in the long grass of the pasture, hunting mice and moles, howling at the moon. *Draw that day the storm broke just after we got the sweet corn in.* She sketched dark clouds, a wall of rain coming in streaks towards the red combine, which was lit up with a pool of god-given light. Some nights he tossed, but if he was still, if he seemed to be really asleep, she'd sketch his bloodless hands, the fingers swollen like sausages.

The stone came to rest on the night he stopped breathing altogether. She had turned the lamp onto his face and gently closed his eyes with the eraser tip of her pencil so they became pools of shadow, as though he slept. She drew the web of deep lines that mapped his features. His hairline, still full around his face. One ear, the tip pressed over from birth.

The stairs behind her creaked, the sound coming down, not going up, ghost-wise. Clem still wondered how her mother knew the sketch was done. She turned to a fresh page, turned the light so her grandfather was in shadow again. Her mother reached over the back of the chair to kiss her hair and squeeze her shoulders.

"I think he died."

She cried into her mother's hand.

She had been seventeen. There were no more summers on the farm.

Her grandmother had a stroke and passed away soon after. The farm was rented out until the rain came and made the land useless. No, she thought, the land had been taken. There were no fields, no corn, no grain or beans to harvest. Just the river everywhere.

TinTin, she noticed, had turned off the car. His head was tilted back, his eyes shut. He squeezed her fingers. She squeezed his hand back. All was quiet, not even the sound of generators. A dream world.

"I have breathed in more of the dirt than I thought. It's the only reason I can think of that would make me feel so bad that it's gone."

Chapter Eight

An Old Tree

Janet Fraser

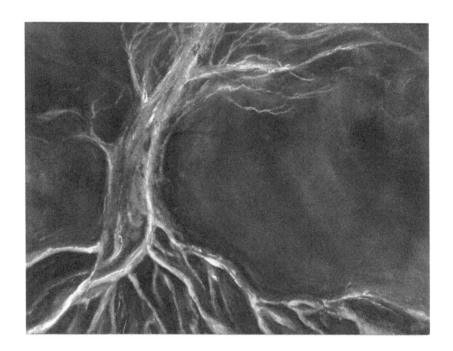

An Old Tree

Blanche MacDonald Markstad

An old tree standing by the windswept road
With broken limbs outstretched
Seeming to hold back the time that has
Upon its branches stretched
The ravage if a thousand years
That left the trunk unharmed
The winter winds have claimed the bark
And torn the mighty arms

Pathetic there it stands amid
The younger and the fair
As if to shout in one last breath
I've known the world. Take care.

Notes on Contributors

Dwayne Avery is an assistant professor in communications studies at Memorial University in Newfoundland.

Renée E. Mazinegiizhigoo-kwe Bédard is of Anishinaabeg ancestry and a member of Dokis First Nation. She holds a PhD from Trent University. Currently, she is an assistant professor at Western University in the Faculty of Eduction. Her area of publication includes work related to topics involving Indigenous mothering, culture and traditions.

Andromeda Bromwich was, at the time of she made her contribution to this book, a twelve year-old girl. She loves modelling, cheerleading, is a Navy cadet, and cares very much about the environment, particularly animals. She is a daughter of Rebecca Bromwich.

Rebecca Jaremko Bromwich is a lawyer, legal academic, mother of four, one-time Green Party parliamentary candidate, and longtime environmental activist.

Karen I. Case is an associate professor in the Department of Education at the University of Hartford.

Janet Fraser is an artist whose home base is Edmonton, Alberta.

Nurcan Atalan-Helicke is an associate professor in Environmental Studies and Sciences Program at Skidmore College.

Blanche MacDonald Markstad was a poet, school teacher and, early European settler in Elk Point, Alberta. She was mother to three and stepmother to four children, all daughters. She passed away in 1976.

Ozcan Ozcevik is a paralegal interested in environmental law.

Noemie Richard is currently completing her second year as an undergraduate honour student studying global and international studies at Carleton University, specializing in global law and social justice.

Josephine Savarese is an associate professor in criminology at St. Thomas University.

Maryellen Symons is an experienced research lawyer with a PhD in philosophy.

Olivia Ungar is a fourth year law and legal studies honours student at Carleton University.

Laura Wythe is a writer, teacher, mother, grandmother, and environmentalist.

Melanie Younger is codirector of the American-based NGO For the Wild, an environmental organization based in deep ecology.

Dara Herman Zierlein is a political artist, born and raised in NYC, and is currently living in Northampton, MA, with her family and animals.

Deepest appreciation to
Demeter's monthly Donors

DEMETER

Daughters
Naomi McPherson
Linda Hunter
Muna Saleh
Summer Cunningham
Rebecca Bromwich
Tatjana Takseva
Kerri Kearney
Debbie Byrd
Laurie Kruk
Fionna Green
Tanya Cassidy
Vicki Noble
Bridget Boland

Sisters
Kirsten Goa
Amber Kinser
Nicole Willey
Regina Edwards